WHAT'S YOUR SQUIRREL I.Q.?

1. How do squirrels remember where they buried their nuts?
2. How do you recognize a real albino squirrel? (Hint: It's not from the color of its fur.)
3. How often do squirrels have babies?
4. Where is the "Squirrel Capital" of America?
5. Where do squirrels go when they die? Stew? Squirrel heaven?

You may be brainier, but you still can't outsmart them. Just be . . .

NUTS ABOUT SQUIRRELS

Answers:

1. They forget where they bury their nuts but they carry little black books containing your name and bird feeder location.

2. True albino squirrels have pink eyes. The common white squirrel just turned that color worrying about humans with brooms.

3. A mother squirrel usually has two litters a year. After birth, it takes four to five weeks before squirrel babies' eyes open and they see what kind of mess they've gotten themselves into.

4. The largest concentration of squirrels in North America is in Washington, D.C., specifically in Lafayette Park, across from the White House, which may or may not influence the mating habits of squirrels.

5. In the wild, most are eaten by predators. The few lucky enough to die from natural causes most likely expire at a bird feeder near a senior center.

NUTS ABOUT SQUIRRELS

A Guide to Coexisting with—and Even Appreciating—Your Bushy-Tailed Friends

RICHARD E. MALLERY

WARNER BOOKS

A Time Warner Company

Warner Books, Inc., 1271 Avenue of the Americas, New York, NY 10020

Visit our Web site at www.twbookmark.com

 A Time Warner Company

Printed in the United States of America

First Printing: September 2000

10 9 8 7 6 5 4 3 2 1

Library of Congress Cataloging-in-Publication Data

Mallery, Richard E.
    Nuts about squirrels : a guide to coexisting with—and even appreciating—
your bushy-tailed friends / Richard E. Mallery.
        p. cm.
    ISBN 0-446-67576-8
    1. Squirrels—Behavior. 2. Squirrels—Humor. I. Title.
QL737.R68 M3315 2000
599.36'15—dc21
                                                                99-086730

Book design and text composition by L & G McRee
Cover design by Diane Luger
Cover illustration by Marc Burkhardt

CONTENTS

PROLOGUE

There are three types of people when it comes to dealing with squirrels. One group is those who are intimidated by their squirrels. Another group is those who imitate their squirrels. The third and most successful group is those who negotiate with their squirrels.

This book will enlighten you as to which group you now belong. By the time you finish this book, you will finally understand that the only successful way of dealing with squirrels and getting on with your life is to negotiate with them.

Once I teach you how a squirrel thinks, you should discover that running around the yard, acting squirrelly, and chasing furballs is a total waste of time. Poor wildlife management skills will never solve your squirrel problems. To resolve your differences, you must achieve a meeting of the minds. A truce must be worked out by both parties involved.

People love to hate their squirrels—or do they? From the thousands of people I have talked to about their squirrels, I find a common thread of appreciation for the little beggars. People like to brag that they have outfoxed their squirrels and banned them from the bird feeder. But in most cases this is just not true. You can fool some of the squirrels all of the time and all of the squirrels some of the time, but you can never fool all of the squirrels all of the time.

Any military strategist will tell you that to be successful in the field, you have to know your opponents. The more you know about the squirrels in your backyard, the more you will appreciate their antics. They have natural abilities that seem to defy gravity. For example, how is it that a squirrel can run out to the very end of a branch that is no more than a spit of sprig and perch there as if in midair while contemplating launching to a bird feeder for lunch?

The more you know squirrels, the less time you will spend trying to outwit them. You will discover a variety of treats they enjoy and are attracted to and will begin to find pleasure in feeding them.

Squirrel feeding has become as popular as feeding wild birds, and whether you like to admit it or not, they are good entertainment. This book should help you and your squirrel find some common ground.

INTRODUCTION

by HAIRY HOUDINI, the Squirrel You Love to Hate

INTERSTATE FLIGHT-ROBBERY

WANTED

FED AND ALIVE

Photograph taken in 1978

HAIRY HOUDINI

DESCRIPTION:

DATE OF BIRTH: UNKNOWN
WEIGHT: 5 TO 6 POUNDS
HEIGHT: 1' 2"
HAIR: YES   EYES: SHIFTY
MO: HIT AND RUN
BUILD: STOCKY   RACE: ALL THE TIME
SCARS AND MARKS: 3 PELLET GUN SCARS ON RIGHT REAR
TATTOOS: "BORN TO BREED" ON LEFT ARM
REMARKS: Frequents backyard bird feeders, and is a known member
of a radical group known to authorities as

"SQUIRRELS FOR AFFIRMATIVE ACTION"
DO NOT ATTEMPT CAPTURE, HE CAN BE
ALARMED AND DANGEROUS

A DICK E. BIRD NEWS PUBLICATION P.O. BOX 377, ACME, MI 49610 COPYRIGHT © 1988

Fact from fiction. Bird feeders across North America are being looted, pillaged, and destroyed by seed-stealing thieves, using guerilla warfare tactics. Hit-'em-and-run maneuvers seem to be their expertise. They are aggressive, destructive, persistent, and annoying. This army survives and flourishes on the food, water, and shelter you provide for the birds in your backyard. They have been observed burying caches of food all over North America in preparation for what experts believe might be a winter offensive. Rodent researchers say these caches of food will give them a second-strike capability as winter food supplies dwindle.

Who are these irksome thieves? These mysterious marauders? Why, they're squirrels, of course.

But we're actually not so bad. In fact, we are among the most interesting and challenging of all backyard wildlife. We are intelligent, inquisitive, skillful, handsome, and exceptional acrobats. Many people get real upset with us little furballs because we eat so much birdseed, and they can't understand why. When bank robber Willie Sutton was once asked why he robbed banks, he said, "Because that's where the money is." Same goes for a squirrel. Opportunity makes a thief. And that's it in a nutshell.

If you knew what us squirrels were saying to you every time you chased us off the feeders or knocked on the window, you would be aghast! Many cute-looking squirrels are very excitable, and many have an R-rated vocabulary. Cross us, and you will always wonder if those little incisors are smiling at you or slyly grinning. You are further ahead if you let squirrels amuse and abuse you. Sharing birdseed with us almost guarantees a peaceful coexistence.

Kiss your birdseed good-bye. It is a combination of goodwill, good-heartedness, and good humor that keeps the bird feeder full even when you know that us good-for-nothing squirrels are going to clean it out the first chance we get. You have to remember, in the depth of your depression over the seed bill, that the birds actually get a little of that seed too! So for the good of all the birds in your yard, for goodness' sake, be good-natured about this issue. Thank goodness God didn't give us little varmints bigger cheeks.

Squirrels trying to eke a living out in your backyard really have it rough. We come from a long line of zigzaggers. Did you ever wonder why us squirrels peek around trees at you and scream obscenities? We have been shot at with various projectiles for centuries. It was bad enough to have

"Be careful, Ernie, the neighbors might have a video camera!"

Native Americans shooting at us with arrows, but then Europeans brought in fire sticks.

At one time we squirrels were such a problem to pioneer farmers, colonies accepted squirrel scalps for payment of taxes. Squirrels turned American crackpots into crack shots. You owe squirrels your freedom. Taking squirrels not only put food on the tables of early settlers of this country, it honed them into riflemen. Colonists who trained their trigger fingers on squirrels devastated the ranks of British soldiers during the American Revolution.

In fact, 40 million squirrels are still killed annually by hunters. That would make anyone peek around a tree before making the big move to the bird feeder. When that tail starts twitching wildly, it is usually a nervous, gun-shy squirrel that has seen a lot of combat.

So come on, why not make a truce with your squirrels? We might eat a little generously, but let's face it, you owe us. You could be drinking heavily taxed tea with your doughnuts. If you have to satisfy an urge to shoot one of us, get yourself one of those battery-operated water guns that rapid-fires at a range up to fifty feet. We have learned to appreciate fire superiority. Some have even begun to show up at the feeders in wet suits.

I do not contend that us squirrels are smarter than humans. We just have a lot of time on our hands and find the temptation of free seed overwhelming. We are goal oriented and, if left to think long and hard enough, will eventually gain access to a bird feeder and eat the entire contents. Squirrels will go in on stilts and hang gliders if they have to—but they will eat your seed.

Many don't mind squirrel baffles and spring-loaded perches on the feeder. These contraptions give some of us a sense of importance. The trouble begins when you start yelling obscenities and knocking at the window while we are trying to enjoy a meal. At this point you are drawing the battle lines. You are telling a squirrel you do not like his company, and you have just made a Big Hairy Deal out of him. Immediately you will begin to see the eye contact, the smirk, the determination welling up inside until his tail shakes and quivers uncontrollably.

This unnatural personality trait has shown up in squirrels from all walks of life. The only way to curb this attitude flaw of epidemic proportions is to establish backyard ground rules. Reduce window knocking and insulting remarks that only fuel the fires of discord. Erect user-friendly baffles that challenge but do not harm squirrels. If your squirrel makes eye contact, look away as if you are unconcerned. It takes practice to be annoyed with a squirrel and not let it show in your body language.

Success is measured in body fat. My father always said, "If a squirrel can see his toes, he's not worth his unsalted peanuts." He taught me young, "If ya can't join 'em, beat

They eat in a hurried nervous rush,
Their eyes are ever darting.
They look for you around the house,
And check windows before starting.

Their tails are jumpy, twitchy, and jerky,
They look as though they're quaking.
Because you yell and threaten them,
They can't tell when you're faking.

They never eat seed at the feeder,
Just stuff it in their cheeks.
They know it's risky eating there,
Because they have no beaks.

They come in colors black to white,
And all those in between.
Their feet are fast, their hands are quick,
And their ears are very keen.

They run and jump and leap and fly
Through branches in the trees.
They never trip, they never fall,
They never scrape their knees.

They chew through wood and plastic,
They gnaw through 12-gauge metal.
Negotiate with them all you want,
But they will never settle.

So if the sun is shining,
Or the snow is in a whirl,
When you look out at your feeder,
There will sit a BIG FAT SQUIRREL!

—DICK E. BIRD

'em." He was from the old school, corn-fed and frugal. He wanted more for me. He said a young squirrel had to specialize if he wanted to get ahead. I studied black oil sunflower seed, and it has provided me with a great living.

But with squirrels there are other dynamics to consider. A squirrel's eyelids are connected directly to the cheek muscles. We use our cheeks as a food warehouse. With the cheeks strained to full capacity, the eyelids are stretched to a point that a squirrel cannot even blink, let alone actuate lids during a sneeze reflex. There may be a grain of truth to the myth that eyes close during a sneeze to keep them from popping out. But a squirrel concentrates more on directing the sneeze through his nasal passage so that he doesn't lose everything in the food warehouse.

Research shows that we forget where we bury our nuts within a half hour. Do you believe this nonsense? If I were that stupid, do you think I could find my way back to your bird feeder every morning? Let me ask you this—When you plant your garden, do you know where every seed is?

Birds eat too darned slow. Their brains have too much time to digest what their beaks are taking in. It's a psychological thing. Their brains tell them they are full before their stomachs have had enough. That's why they are flittin' back and forth all the time.

A squirrel works totally differently. A squirrel doesn't have a brain that's always buttin' in where it's not wanted. A squirrel's brain and a squirrel's stomach work on two different shifts. The stomach works on the day shift and will tell the squirrel he is full, if he ever is. The brain is nocturnal; it lets the squirrel think about seed all night long until the stomach finally wakes up and goes back to work.

When a squirrel buries a nut, it's usually in his stomach. We just make it look like we are burying it in the ground to drive researchers crazy. The researchers keep putting out more nuts for us to bury, and everyone is happy!

Just to prove how little you actually know about us, I will quote from a recent study done on squirrels like myself.

"Individual squirrels consume about two pounds of food per week, or one hundred pounds a year." Get real! I eat more than that for breakfast on any given day.

Many people make the mistake of chasing their squirrels. This only makes us eat more. A squirrel's body is at peak performance at a certain intake level. When a squirrel is chased off the bird feeder and has to run all the time, he burns a ton of calories. These calories have to be replaced, which brings the squirrel back to the bird feeder. It's a vicious circle.

My advice to people who feed birds and are annoyed by squirrels is: Never, and I mean *never*, let them see you sweat.

I never met a squirrel

I didn't like.

—HAIRY HOUDINI

NUTS ABOUT SQUIRRELS

CHAPTER ONE

Squirrel Biographies

Squirrels get a lot of attention because, like songbirds, they have become our closest wildlife connection. They are gifted with senses we cannot understand and live by a natural calling we will never hear. They are a perfectly finished extension of the natural world turned tame by civilization. They patronize us for our handouts and scold us with contempt for our greed.

The main characters at North American bird feeders representing the Sciuridae crime family include various brands of chipmunks, ground squirrels, and tree squirrels. Three on the most-wanted list would include the gray, fox, and red squirrels. The whole Sciuridae family shares the same addiction—birdseed!

That a squirrel's diet relies heavily on the eating, gathering, and storing of acorns is not groundbreaking news. To a squirrel, the acorn is the Wonder Bread that builds strong bodies twelve ways. The acorn can be opened and eaten in less than half the time needed for other, harder nuts. But how the squirrel's diet influences its habitat is quite interesting. Some studies show that gray squirrels fail to recover up to 80 percent of the seeds they bury. A squirrel's poor memory, or planned landscaping, aids in the regeneration of forests in North America.

Squirrels, along with blue jays and a few other small animals, are important in maintaining and regenerating second-growth forests and may even have been responsible for spreading the vast stands of timber once found throughout North America. Like politicians, squirrels and jays will steal from each other in a vicious circle. The squirrel will bury a seed while the jay spies. The jay will fly down, uncover the seed, and fly off to cache it himself. The squirrel will run up the tree and steal it back. Eventually, some of these well-traveled seeds will turn into a tree or a shrub that the squirrels and blue jays will both use for food and shelter.

During the winter months, a squirrel's main diet consists of nuts and seeds—much of that being birdseed. Active throughout the year, the squirrel stores large quantities of food to see him through the winter. This might seem a huge waste of time, with all the food programs being run by bird lovers in North America. But the squirrel cannot rely solely on charity at the bird feeder to get him through a hard winter. Even though the squirrel eats 100 percent of your income, he is only getting about 20 percent of his food source from you.

Some researchers feel that squirrel habits are changing in urban populations where handouts (or, more appropriately, takeouts) are available year-round. The squirrel is one of the few wild animals that has adapted to humans and learned to coexist with sometimes irate homeowners. Squirrels can live comfortably on natural foods and the variety of free fare they find around nicely landscaped yards. Not only do they enjoy the many food items left out for songbirds, they also love the exotic plants used for landscaping and gardening. A squirrel is an opportunist when it comes to diet. Whatever you sow, a squirrel will reap.

Some squirrels are scatter hoarders, burying and hiding gathered food in hundreds of locations, while others build one large cache. It depends whether they favor the old saying, "Don't put all your eggs in one basket," or Mark Twain's version, "Put all your eggs in one basket and watch that basket."

Are squirrels afraid of the dark? During the summer squirrels are most active a few hours after sunrise and a few hours before sunset. During the day a squirrel will often find an inconspicuous branch to stretch out on. He lies on his belly, letting his feet hang down and head rest pointing straight out. Being opportunistic, he will come out of this afternoon slumber if food presents itself. Squirrels retire to their nests before nightfall and very  seldom venture out after dark. Are they afraid of the dark? You're darned right they are. Except for the flying squirrel, which has eyes adapted to night foraging, most squirrels know that they are no match for owls, coyotes, and many other predawn predators out looking for a midnight snack.

A hollowed-out tree cavity or a man-made nesting box would be a squirrel's first choice in filling his housing needs. These locations are called dens. More often, because of lack of habitat, squirrels end up building dreys— bundled leaf structures that protect them from mild weather conditions.

Ground squirrels live subterraneously in a burrow, while tree squirrels live in tree cavities or dreys. So to decide what type of squirrel you have, first find out if it has a burrow or a balcony. Nest building usually takes less than a day; squirrels much prefer to forage and eat.

In the winter squirrels are out even less. In an attempt to conserve energy, they forage the first half of the day and then lie low until the next day. In severe cold and heavy winter storms, squirrels will curl up in their nests for days. Like Garbo, squirrels "vant to be alone." But on a freezing cold day in the middle of winter, they don't mind snuggling with a neighbor on occasion.

Squirrels do not experience a utopian lifestyle all winter, living off the fat of the land in blissful slumber. When many people do not see their squirrels for a few days, they think they must be hibernating. Actually, squirrels experience long bouts of insomnia. Same is true for the little chipmunks that take good-sized chunks of your birdseed output and burrow under your house with them. Chipmunks fill an underground vault with the birdseed void in your life and slumber near it all winter. This is not true hibernation; chipmunks will wake up several times in the middle of winter. Scientists do not know if they have to get up and go to the bathroom, need midwinter snacks, or just have bad dreams. One researcher thinks that this behavior might be to warm their brains. Cold brains do not sleep well, and stoking the metabolic woodstove might help the chippies snooze better. Chipmunks need a good winter's sleep because during the spring and summer they use enormous amounts of energy, running up and down bird-feeder poles with cheeks ballooned to capacity with birdseed.

Members of the squirrel family differ from other small rodents in a number of ways. Their sense of sight is much more developed because of their daylight activities. A squirrel's eyes are much larger than those of other rodents because he is always so surprised to see how much seed you have put out for him. It also has to do with his need to stay on constant guard for predators. With his eyes wide apart on the sides of his head, a squirrel does not have binocular vision. This lack of depth perception means that a squirrel must swivel his head from side to side before making a move. So when people yell at a squirrel to get off the bird

**"I called the Psychic Friends 900 number, Bea.
They said I was going to meet a lot of new friends!"**

feeder and the squirrel shakes his head no, he is actually
just compensating for his limited frontal vision.

What I have always found amazing is that a squirrel
never bites his tongue. Unlike other fast eaters, a squirrel
has a very coordinated mouth. He rips his food apart,
chews at lightning speed, stuffs his cheeks to beyond ca-

pacity, and scans a 360-degree view, all at the same time, never making that painful mistake we all have experienced. While all this activity is going on, the squirrel is using his tongue to position food under his molars for grinding. Just once, you would think you would hear a painful little whimper come from him just to prove he isn't perfect.

If you have ever watched a squirrel eating a sap-sticky fresh pinecone, you have witnessed the most efficient eater in the natural world. Holding the pinecone in his front paws, the squirrel peels the individual cone scales back like a banana peel and eats each seed before peeling the next scale back. This is all done in record time, as if each fresh pinecone were part of a relay race.

You have to appreciate where squirrels are coming from. I don't mean from trees; I mean how they have become expert tree traversers. Getting to your seed is not a problem for critters that have spent the last few million years running through the tops of trees and feeding on flimsy figments of fir.

Studies show that squirrels have great memories. No, they don't always remember where they buried their nuts, but they do carry little black books with your name in them. They grade you from 1 to 10. If you offered good seed with easy access, you are a 10 and listed under Easy. These are reference guides that squirrels do not share with other squirrels.

Research shows that a gray squirrel can jump up, down, and sideways. It can hang on to whatever it can land on, and if it misses by a couple inches, no problem. It will just readjust its windage and elevation, reset its sights, and fire again. So most squirrels that look as if they are baffled by spring-loaded feeder devices are actually only joyriding.

Whatever type of squirrel you are observing, you will find it has the same work ethic—Work hard, never stop. It doesn't matter what season of the year it is, squirrels are thrifty. Tree squirrels as well as ground squirrels will hoard food and cache it away. Tree squirrels do not hibernate during the winter like many ground squirrels. They stay active and hole up only when the weather turns brutal.

If there were child support laws in the animal kingdom, male squirrels would be in court instead of the courtyard on a regular basis. The male will breed with several females, but that is where his parental duties stop. The female will raise the young, taking up to ten weeks to wean them. Squirrel milk is a very rich source of nutrients, and the little furballs grow very quickly.

In captivity squirrels have been known to live eighteen to twenty years, but in the wild a majority never celebrate their first birthday parties. Squirrels get little protection even from wildlife managers sworn to protect them. I have always found it odd that authorities will permit a homeowner to shoot a supposedly nuisance squirrel at the drop of a hat, but then bust a homeowner who has taken in an orphaned baby squirrel to raise.

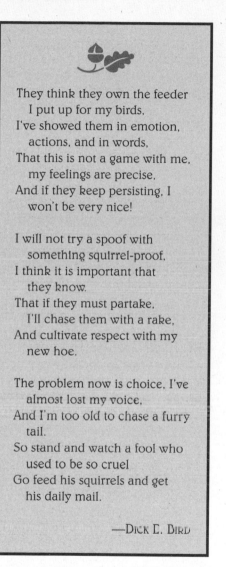

They think they own the feeder
  I put up for my birds,
I've showed them in emotion,
  actions, and in words,
That this is not a game with me,
  my feelings are precise,
And if they keep persisting, I
  won't be very nice!

I will not try a spoof with
  something squirrel-proof,
I think it is important that
  they know.
That if they must partake,
  I'll chase them with a rake,
And cultivate respect with my
  new hoe.

The problem now is choice, I've
  almost lost my voice,
And I'm too old to chase a furry
  tail.
So stand and watch a fool who
  used to be so cruel
Go feed his squirrels and get
  his daily mail.

—DICK E. BIRD

A gray squirrel is not as large as the fox squirrel, but it's not because he isn't trying. If you watch the two species, you will see that they are constantly trying to outeat one another, usually at your expense. The gray does not have as fluffy a tail, but his ears are more pointed, and he has a much sharper tongue.

The most common type of squirrel in North America, the gray squirrel can range in color from light gray, tan, or brownish to darker browns and black. There are also white phases (without albino characteristics) and albino colonies in several states.

It is almost impossible to describe a range for the eastern gray squirrel because it has been introduced to so many western regions, and its natural eastern range has extended through bird-feeder head-start lunch programs offered by thousands of backyard bird-feeding enthusiasts all across North America.

Depending on food availability, gray squirrels will often have two litters per year. The gestation period is just under fifty days, usually spring and late summer. Litter sizes average three to four, and it takes the naked young nine to ten weeks to turn into a certified, seed-stealing furball.

The average gray squirrel is fifteen inches long and weighs about one pound. His diet consists mainly of nuts, seeds, and fruit, but he will eat scraps from the trash, including bread, meat, and even snack foods. Gray squirrels will eat young birds and birds' eggs, but not as often as the feisty red squirrel. Like all squirrels, the gray is an opportunist and will eat whatever the season offers: nuts, seeds, insects, fungi, buds and berries, even carrion. High mortality rate in urban squirrels is due not so much to predators but rather to automobiles. By contrast, their rural counterparts often perish from starvation.

The most common squirrel in the Northwest is the nonnative eastern gray squirrel, which was introduced to the Seattle area in the early 1900s and has become well established in urban and suburban areas. Recent studies show that there are muggers in this group of wild westerners: gray squirrels have been observed stalking and pouncing on unsuspecting quail. The bird seemed to be minding his own business when a squirrel, waiting on a nearby stump, pounced on him.

"Hey, we have a time share on this unit."

Biologists are convinced that this is not an isolated incident. Other victims of the gray squirrel include other birds, lots of rabbits, reptiles, mice, and possibly even other squirrels. Studies have shown that tree squirrels in British Columbia knock off a good number of snowshoe hare youngsters, that ground squirrels prey on other burrowers like moles and gophers, and that chipmunks indulge on lizards.

Here is the real kicker. Biologists are thinking that the squirrels are not after the meat; they want the bones of these other critters. It may be just a supplement to their diet, but it is pretty evident that some squirrels have skeletons in their closets.

Gray squirrels build large nests of leaves and twigs on tree branches, or they den within tree cavities and in buildings where they can gain access through open spaces in the roof, attic, or walls.

Fox squirrels, the largest tree squirrels in North America, are considered by some the most handsome. The coat of the fox squirrel is usually lush reddish tan with a light belly. Like the gray, fox squirrels can vary in color from white/gray to brown/black. They average in size over two pounds in weight and two feet in length.

Like the gray squirrel, the fox has been introduced to the western states and had its eastern range extended through human activities. I have seen fox squirrels in northern hardwoods and southern cypress swamps.

The omnivorous fox squirrel enjoys a good flower bulb whenever he thinks you have put some out for him. He also enjoys natural cuisine, like seeds, nuts, berries, fruits, tree bark and buds, insects, eggs, and fungi.

Litter size, gestation, and weaning mirror that of the gray squirrel. Also, like the gray squirrel, the fox will typically build a tree nest in the summer and look for a cavity nest in the winter, even if it means sharing a compartment with another semihibernating nonbather. Like other rodents, fox squirrels are accomplished gnawers, using their sharp, ever-growing front teeth to strip bark and chew through wood and plastic.

Breeding season begins in late winter and, depending on conditions and food availability, squirrels may produce two litters a year. The average litter size is three babies, born naked and blind. Young fox squirrels remain in the nest for about six weeks.

Many orchard farmers target the fox squirrel as a crop destroyer. But the fox squirrel is just innocently trying to share the bounty. He has no clue that all that fruit is future pie filling meant for already overweight humans.

Red squirrels are about half the size of gray squirrels. They are little, but they are mighty. Their ears are smaller, but they sport hair tufts. The red squirrel's tail is smaller, less fluffy, and flatter than that of both the gray and the fox. His name pretty much describes his coloring—reddish brown to rust but with a light-colored belly. In the summer, the red squirrel looks a little gray on the back. This light summer coat becomes much heavier in the fall and winter, and much redder. Fighting weight for a red squirrel is only about a half pound, but he makes up for what he lacks in bulk with a ferocious appetite for life. When I exaggerate about squirrels' eating anything that doesn't eat them first, I am usually referring to red squirrels. Besides eating everything on the regular squirrel menu, they are also known to attack and eat other mammals, such as young rabbits and squirrels.

One consistent squirrel tale is that the brutal little red squirrel will chase down the mild-mannered gray and castrate him at every opportunity. There is no truth to this vicious rumor, which has perpetuated itself because the red squirrel has such a demonic attitude. In reality, the sober-minded gray squirrel will usually yield right-of-way to the pushy little red squirrel. Gray squirrels would rather switch than fight.

The red squirrel usually has just one litter per year, but bears twice as many young as her larger cousins. The red squirrel prefers a leaf nest but will use a bird's nest, tree, or ground cavity.

When breaking and entering, red squirrels will often work as a gang. I have livetrapped as many as eight out of one building. I once gave my father a large bag of thistle seed for Christmas. When he left for Florida for the winter, he left his thistle seed behind, and the red squirrels zeroed in on it immediately. When I discovered the break-in, I set a live trap and captured three suspects. I then vacuumed the room and cleaned up the mess. The next day I found that the vacuum bag had a large gaping hole in it, and seed was scattered all over the house again. I captured five more red squirrels in two days, and finally the party was over.

American Indians have many legends about the squirrel. One of them tells why the small red squirrel bursts into sputtering, scolding, snapping, and foot stomping while furiously twitching his tail whenever he sees man: once upon a time, it seems, an old Indian brave, with divine permission, reduced the red squirrel from an enormous animal to his present diminutive size.

The red squirrel is a chatterbox of scold when irritated. He can be a ruthless bully. His approach at the bird feeder is one of authority. It doesn't matter how big you are; it's what ya do with what ya got! Twenty years ago, our highest-ranking military man was Admiral McCain. He was just a little guy. When his car went by, all you could see was his cigar sticking up out of the backseat of his chauffeured Lincoln. But he was smarter than everyone else, a little feisty, and ended up with five stars when everyone else had only four. The same goes for the red squirrel. He thinks he has five stars; and when he barks out orders, everyone stands tall.

"Chickaree" is a common name for the red squirrel in many parts of the country. This name comes from the cry the red squirrel utters. There are other cries in his territory too, usually from some poor soul that crossed paths with him, or just plain crossed him.

Red squirrels are connoisseurs of fine nuts but will also partake of any bird eggs, new plant shoots, young birds, or a well-managed bird feeder. Almost everything available is food to a red squirrel. Many people think a red squirrel eats solely at the bird feeder, but actually he spends a lot of time eating seeds of pine, spruce, and balsam trees, nuts and acorns, mushrooms, buds, sap, berries, bark, and bird's eggs.

Red squirrels are a very important part of backyard bird feeding. This redhead can gnaw through wood and plastic feeders faster than a hot knife through warm butter. If we did not have these little furballs, our feeders would last forever and we would never get any new and more exciting models. Many experts say that gray squirrels do most feeder damage, but I believe this is just a vicious rumor started by a bunch of red squirrels. Most red squirrels are hyperactive and major grain grabbers. They can put big dents in your seed supply if you do not yell at them on a regular basis.

These small squirrels are very versatile in their housing needs too. You can find them in abandoned woodpecker holes, outside in nests of leaves and twigs, in the ground, or in fancy nesting boxes you have mounted for songbirds.

What you have heard about redheads having a short fuse can be easily proven when dealing with your red squirrel. A red squirrel has a very nasty mouth on him. It is probably best that you do not understand what he is saying. Often you will see him chasing away much larger squirrels that dare trespass in a feeder on his turf.

Even though red squirrels can be a bit obnoxious, they can be easily tamed. During the early part of the twentieth century, many squirrels were sold as pets. In some cases, the unscrupulous seller would not want to take the time to tame the animals before he sold them. The squirrels would be drugged and sold under the influence as tame and easily handled. When the squirrels finally came around, the salesman and the squirrels would be long gone.

Red squirrels are among the most common of all North American squirrels. They range as far north as trees grow. Where you find trees, you usually find red squirrels. Just ask the family in Ontario who brought one into the house on their Christmas tree. For days, they could not figure out who was opening the presents. At first, they thought it was a mouse. They never thought to look into the tree branches. Red squirrels love to eat Christmas foods, like nuts, grains, and fruit—now we can add candy canes to the list!

Flying squirrel. The skin flap that allows this mammal, which is similar in size and color to the red squirrel, to glide is connected to its front and back legs. When the squirrel does a spread-eagle, the gliding membrane tightens and acts as a parasail.

"Are you sure this thing is going to work?"

Flying squirrels are very thin-skinned, and I don't mean personality-wise. Their abundance of thinly furred skin between the front and back legs is what enables them to glide. This membrane almost triples the area of the squirrel's underbody, allowing him to glide up to fifty yards. The squirrel can make directional changes during his glide by working the muscles of his membrane. He often does this to outmaneuver an owl, his chief predator. Just before landing, the flying squirrel drops his tail and lifts his front feet, which creates slack in the flight skin. This serves as an air brake, which prevents a neck break. He actually lands very gently on all fours and immediately scurries around to make sure no one is following him.

A flying squirrel will set sap-tap traps. Like the red squirrel, he enjoys tree sap. The flying squirrel will also eat many moths that are attracted to the sap.

These squirrels are mostly nocturnal fliers. They have very large eyes for night vision. They will glide up to 150 feet. If you have ever had one land near you after dark, the first thought is usually—bat. Flying squirrels are actually gliders, not fliers, but they are very quick. I had one in my travel trailer one night, and I couldn't get near him. It was like chasing a billiard ball around a table. I finally opened the door, and when his bounce angle was finally right, he fell out. I don't know if his little nocturnal eyes were always that big, or just when he ran into half-naked people headed for the bathroom in the dark.

Flying squirrels are larder hoarders. Like other squirrels, the flying squirrel has an attraction to anything that has to do with eating, and finds a multitude of natural food appealing. I have had them fill my bluebird nesting boxes right to the gills with dried mushrooms in the fall and move into the nesting box next door. They are tree-cavity nesters, and like to be close to their groceries. I have one that lives in a nesting box attached to a utility pole. When disturbed, the squirrel darts out of the box and instantly disappears. It takes a quick eye to follow the squirrel up to the top of the pole, where he sails off to a group of thick conifers.

Flying squirrels are common throughout much of the United States and Canada, though they are not found in some of the prairie states and the Southwest. They are very gentle animals. If you have nesting boxes for birds, you will often find they have set up residence in one.

Never feed the hand that bites you. Squirrels can be alarmed and dangerous. The most common confrontational problem with wildlife is a squirrel bite. This usually happens when a person is trying to feed a squirrel by hand. If you are going to feed a furball, lay the food in the palm of your hand, not between the fingers. A squirrel dedicates his eyesight to scanning for predators and lunch menu items. This leaves very little focus on fingers. Often, the squirrel cannot tell where the peanut butter sandwich stops and the fingers start.

A squirrel gives new definition to the term *finger food*. In the case of a squirrel bite, do not lance the wound and suck the poison out; squirrels are not vipers. The most important step is to rinse the wound immediately and wash it thoroughly with soap and water. If you haven't had a tetanus shot in a few years, now would be the time to get one. The risk of rabies from a furball is almost nil.

There are cases where squirrels have gone on rampages and terrorized whole communities. In Westerville, Ohio, more than one gray squirrel attacked at least eight people. The furry suspects with beady eyes had taken over a tree-lined neighborhood, and no one felt safe. Police once had to set up traps, send out patrols, and even corner suspects in the county park, but no arrests were ever made; police were unable to nab any of the suspected squirrels. One officer, while on patrol, witnessed an attack. The squirrel appeared friendly but suddenly leaped at the victim and bit her leg. Unprovoked attacks like this lasted two weeks during the spring, then suddenly ended as quickly as they began. This case remains a mystery to this day, but like many unsolved cases, it may have a lot to do with spring and hormones.

The *London Mirror* once slandered New York City squirrels, alleging that Central Park squirrels had become drug crazed from eating half-empty vials of crack tossed by addicts. Supposedly, lunchtime strollers were being attacked by nutty furballs. Park officials denied that any such thing had taken place. There is little if any drug use among Central Park squirrels, they said; there was one stakeout, but the park rangers had been given a bad tip. All they found was one raccoon with an overactive thyroid and a half-eaten Twinkie. The New York Parks Department made it very clear that its squirrels have no bloodshot eyes, no dilated pupils, and scamper in straight lines.

The *New York Times* fired back, "Yes, they scamper and frolic, but they're not high."

I personally have known squirrels with five-pound-a-day cracked corn habits, but I have never heard of a squirrel stupid enough to take a mind-altering drug.

• • •

Squirrels are rarely the aggressors. Many a dog will instinctively kill a squirrel if he can snag one. President Bush's dog, Millie, gave the press corps the impression she was the White House killer dog. She loved to chase squirrels. The president even encouraged it. Without the president's prodding, Millie was actually very mellow, maybe even yellow. One day, a squirrel turned on Millie, and she turned tail and ran for the nearest Secret Service agent.

The flip side to this behavior would be Queenie, a laid-back terrier from southern California. Queenie wanted a family real bad, but when she finally had a pup, it didn't survive. At the same time an orphaned squirrel was brought into the house. Queenie adopted the little furball and was soon nursing the squirrel and glowing like a new mom.

Dogs have always been thought to be natural enemies of the squirrel. Poor Millie was forced to perpetuate that fallacy. But Queenie, the terrier, broke down the barrier and let the truth of the matter prevail. Squirrels and dogs can live in peace.

I am not saying that all dogs love squirrels. I am just saying that it can be an alternative lifestyle. Granted, Queenie is from California and most likely raised on free love, good vibrations, and a mindset of sunglow, while Millie was a Washington-fed, Texas-bred media darling that had to perform on cue. She was not afraid of squirrels when she was surrounded by marines and half the Secret Service. She knew that these people were instructed to jump on her and use their bodies to shield her from any danger. But this is not the normal relationship of dog and squirrel. Let your dog make up his own mind!

Food and fun are never absent from a squirrel's thoughts. Squirrels love festivities. They have joined in on more than one Easter egg hunt. The tradition of hiding colorful eggs for kids to find has caught on in the squirrel realm. Squirrels don't seem to mind if the eggs are real or plastic, they just take pleasure in the hunt. Christmas is the same way. Many homeowners find their Christmas decorations missing and can't imagine who would do such a thing.

One year at the zoo in Tulsa, Oklahoma, officials decided on a "ZooLIGHTful" theme during the Christmas holidays. They put up 130,000 Christmas lights, which really turned the squirrels on. Within hours, the squirrels began to drag the six- and eight-foot sections of lights back to their nests. They were really getting into the Christmas spirit and were streaming by with decorations and fighting over the most colorful bulbs. It was almost as chaotic as Macy's the day after Christmas.

The following year, zoo officials treated the lights with VapoRub, pepper spray, and deodorant. It slowed the squirrel light-theft down, and there were fewer chest colds, but all the squirrels around the Tulsa Zoo that year were half lit.

• • •

How far have squirrels come in adjusting to urban development? I'm not asking about their ability to navigate baffled bird feeders and forage for food in a sterile environment. I am talking about developing techniques to survive the crush of humanity on their habitat and how they have come to cope.

We are constantly making jokes about squirrels crossing the road. I don't know how the chicken ever got top billing. The squirrel has always found it more challenging. Our opinion of squirrel intelligence is lopsided because we only see the results of failure, the agony of defeat, and never the triumph of victory and success. There is no sign of the squirrels that successfully negotiate the busy highway, day after day.

One success story deals with a Minnesota gray squirrel that lives in a Twin Cities park near a very busy intersection. This squirrel waits for the "Walk" light to come on and then crosses the street, maintaining a polite distance from the other pedestrians. Once the squirrel collects what he is after, he crosses back to the park, but not always by the same route. Sometimes he circles the whole intersection, waiting each time to cross only when the "Walk" light illuminates.

Many squirrels do not make the right career moves and end up flat and broke. Given the circumstances, however, squirrel populations have done very well, even in congested and increasingly rapidly developing urban areas.

Another story involves a Douglas squirrel. A bit smaller than gray or fox squirrels, Douglas squirrels range through the Sierras from Mexico to British Columbia—but one, dubbed Walla Walla, tried to extend his range to Alaska. Walla Walla apparently "squirreled away" in a U.S. Postal Service shipping container that left Seattle. The little guy went first-class to Fairbanks, where he came down the sort line with insufficient postage. Mail sorters in Fairbanks thought the squirrel had just wandered into the building.

A postal facility is not a squirrel-friendly place. Besides all the conveyor belts and sorting machinery, a lot of postal workers carry guns. At first, the postal employees tried to shoo the squirrel out a door. But Walla Walla was no dummy. It was 15 degrees below zero, with about nine inches of snow on the ground. He refused to go outside.

Walla Walla was able to find plenty of food by shopping through packages in the various shipping containers stored around the facility. When Alaska Fish and Game personnel were finally called in to capture the squirrel, he was trapped in a container headed for Prudhoe Bay. That would have been a big mistake. He was a little snappy, but I guess that's what happens when you hang around a postal facility for a couple days.

Once captured, Walla Walla did not resemble the reddish brown squirrels of Fairbanks. Fish and Game checked his pelt with specimens at the University of Alaska Museum and confirmed that Walla Walla was a Douglas squirrel. Since this species is protected in Washington State, Fish and Game felt obligated by law to return the squirrel. First they named him after Walla Walla, Washington, a city in his home range. He dined on yams, fruit, and peanuts while officials booked him onto an Alaskan Airlines flight back to Seattle. He was given ambassador treatment. When his plane touched down in Seattle, he was met by Fish and Game employees there, who then escorted him to Governor Mike Lowry's mansion at the state capital in Olympia, Washington.

Walla Walla became something of a star. He was never invited to dinner, but then when did a squirrel ever need an invitation? The governor's mansion is an officially designated Backyard Wildlife Sanctuary, and Walla Walla was used to draw attention to the BWS program, which allows homeowners to obtain the sanctuary designation if they agree to certain conditions to help maintain birds, animals, and plants native to the state. No matter how nice you are to your squirrels, however, you still cannot claim them as dependents on your state income tax.

**"With the new surcharge, do you suppose stealing
seed will be considered tax fraud?"**

Population implosion. Contrary to popular belief, the
number of squirrels is declining. This is mostly due to loss
of habitat. Squirrels only seem more abundant because we
keep compressing them into smaller and smaller living
areas, as we have with all of nature. Squirrels have become
very adaptable to living in close quarters with humans.
They realize by now that they are not always welcome.
They used to run in herds, and now they run when you are
heard. We have taken away much of the squirrel's heritage
and, without realizing it, turned him into a common beggar.

Most squirrels know by now that the goodies you put
out to attract songbirds are not meant for them. When they
climb around all of your engineering and eat everything you

put forth, they are only trying to make you understand that they do not care what you think!

I can't believe they ate the whole thing! Squirrels never know when to stop. After years of research, it is well documented that squirrels have eyes much bigger than their stomachs. The nerve endings between the squirrel's stomach and brain are very primitive and poorly developed. This causes him to eat far beyond his capacity before the brain receives any message to shut down the jaw muscles.

There is an upside to having hordes of hoarding rodents visit your bird feeder on a regular basis. The main advantage is that you never have to clean the feeder; any squirrel worth his salt will destroy a bird feeder long before it ever has a chance to become dirty. Sharks feed in a frenzy, but squirrels feed in a frantic. They know that if the birds find out that you have just filled the feeder, it will draw a crowd. So they always try to make it look like it's about empty by eating two-thirds of it right away.

Squirrels are usually on an unbalanced diet—they eat too much, too often. It's the American way. Cardiac problems are responsible for about 50 percent of all squirrel deaths. Just plain car problems are responsible for the rest.

One thing squirrels have going for them is the fact that they get plenty of exercise. They lead very busy lives and can actually burn off calories while they are eating. If you study squirrels, you will notice that their jaws move faster than the wing of a hummingbird. This constant, rapid motion takes an enormous amount of energy. It takes one sunflower seed out of every two just to fuel the jaw muscles that process the tons of intake a squirrel annually digests. Because of the volume their jaw muscles are capable of handling, these rodents have developed expandable cheeks, which have evolved naturally from being stressed to their maximum capacity. Most squirrels can hold twice their own weight in each cheek, which does distort the face considerably, causing them to look congested. An overextended squirrel is unable to close his eyelids because the facial tissue is stretched too far, restricting lid actuation and causing the eyes to look bigger than the stomach.

AFTER

I went from a size 10 to a size 24 in three short weeks on this diet, and I feel terrific. I've tried many diets, but Ultra Corn Gain Fast is the only thing that worked. I feel like a new squirrel. In fact, I feel like two new squirrels. I've been skinny all my life, but now with UCGF, and all the feeders folks are putting out for me, I know I'll never be skinny again. UCGF made it so easy for me to put on weight, I will never take it off. My results were extraordinary. I highly recommend this diet to squirrels all over North America. One squirrel raised his cholesterol 238 points!

BEFORE

I always worried about my weight. I tried all kinds of diets, but they all left me feeling tired and depressed. Then I discovered Ultra Corn Gain Fast. I was amazed how easy it was. I didn't feel like I was on a diet, never hungry or deprived. I began gaining weight immediately. All these new squirrel feeders around the country give me all the energy I need to keep up with my hectic schedule. Best of all, I haven't felt as skinny as this old picture of me since UCGF came into my life. UCGF is a major breakthrough in controlling weight and increasing cholesterol.

Review and Relate

- Squirrel ears face to the sides like ours do. Mouse and rat ears face forward.
- Squirrels chatter and generally make a great deal more noise than other members of the rodent family. And the variety of sounds is much greater too.
- The gray squirrel is more of a lover than a fighter and will often let red squirrels and woodpeckers run him off the premises.
- When a squirrel senses danger, his first instinct is to stand motionless. His second instinct is to swallow hard and chew faster.
- The vain male squirrel takes twice as much time to groom himself as does the female.
- The animal warden in Fredericksburg, Virginia, was once called in to break up a squirrel brawl. It seems that four little baby squirrels had their tails entangled, and they all wanted to branch out in different directions. A local vet was able to figure out the squirrelly knot and separate them.
- Squirrels communicate through a series of chirps and tail-flagging. The frequency and the duration of their tail-flagging communicate everything from panic to picnics. Sounds are used in conjunction with tail and other gestures.
- The sweat glands of a tree squirrel are located on its feet and paws. When hot or excited, a squirrel will sweat all over your bird feeder. Sweating is also a squirrelly method of marking territorial trees.
- If a squirrel's nest becomes infested with fleas or other insects, he will move to or build a new nest.
- Squirrels will build nests in unusual places—attics, automobiles, woodstoves, barbecue grills, even power boxes.
- Contrary to popular belief, squirrels do not hibernate. They are less active in the winter, which is a survival tactic. It is believed that squirrels eat a lot just prior to a storm, which makes sense—every day is prior to a storm,

"If it's so easy, you go find nuts!"

and squirrels eat a lot every day. Then they spend stormy days in their nests, watching soap operas and eating black oil sunflower seeds.

- City squirrels have smaller territories than country squirrels. Like humans, urban squirrels have to share resources and try to get along with their neighbors. Squirrels in the country are more independent and defend their territories with much more vigor.
- If a squirrel thinks he is being watched, he will hide food temporarily or pretend to be hiding food, then move it to a more secure or convenient location. This is called the bait-and-switch.
- Too many salted peanuts could cause your squirrel to have high blood pressure. This, in turn, can cause an early death. Yelling at your squirrel can also cause high blood pressure.

"When he gets really mad he can yell 140 words a minute, with gusts up to 180!"

- The North American Council on Biological Formulation has signed an agreement among all country members that squirrel cloning will not be allowed.
- No squirrel is an island.
- A squirrel by any other name is still a seed-stealing thief.
- There are about 300 different kinds of squirrels, including the red squirrel, gray squirrel, fox squirrel, and flying squirrel. In addition, chipmunks, prairie dogs, woodchucks, and groundhogs are also considered squirrelly neighbors to most people.
- I don't mean to scare you, but squirrels are rodents. The order Rodentia is one of the fastest growing families in the world, since rodents are among the fastest breeding of all animals. The squirrel population in your yard is

growing as you sit here reading this excellent book. When your squirrels are not sitting on your bird feeder, filling their cheeks to beyond capacity, they are at family-planning meetings.

- The order Rodentia includes squirrels, prairie dogs, woodchucks, porcupines, muskrats, beaver, rats, and mice. When they smile at you with their chisel-shaped incisor teeth, you know they love you.
- A squirrel's tail, designed for balance, is so effective that it can make some humans unbalanced.
- Squirrels are great snow tunnelers when deep snow makes it necessary.
- Your phone bill is inflated because of squirrels for two reasons. You call friends to tell them the unbelievable things they do, and they cause millions of dollars worth of cable damage annually, which ends up on your bill in the long distance.
- Squirrels have acute vision, acute hearing, and acute little face.
- Squirrels are very protective parents. One was observed boxing a hawk. Between the noise and the left hook, the hawk finally fled.

Tree Rat Trivia

Things You Should Know about Squirrels

1. Is it legal to keep a squirrel as a pet?
2. Why do squirrels hide food in so many locations?
3. Does a squirrel live the life of Riley?
4. What pixielike name does the red squirrel also go by?
5. What is the average life span of a squirrel?

Things You Thought You Knew about Squirrels

1. What is the gliding membrane on a flying squirrel called?
2. Can flying squirrels see in complete darkness?
3. Do squirrels smell bad?

4. When does a young squirrel develop claws?

5. How much food does a squirrel really eat?

THINGS YOU WISH YOU NEVER KNEW ABOUT SQUIRRELS

1. What is the best way to keep a squirrel from eating your birdseed?

2. What did Native Americans think of squirrels?

3. What gift did early American colonists receive from tree squirrels?

4. Can a squirrel wiggle his ears?

5. Does a squirrel have to worry about underarm odor?

Trivia Answers

Things you should know about squirrels: 1. Most cities, counties, and states have rules about keeping wild animals as pets, and permits are often required. It is not a good idea. Squirrels make lousy pets and were designed to live outdoors on bird feeders. 2. Because they learned a long time ago not to put all their eggs in one basket. If another animal finds their cache, they don't lose a whole season's rations. 3. Squirrels get into bird feeders on a regular basis, which gives the impression they are laid-back free-loaders. But a squirrel's life is no picnic. Squirrels have many enemies besides the broom-wielding madmen who hide around the corners of houses waiting to ambush them. Bobcats, cats, dogs, coyotes, foxes, hawks, owls, snakes, and weasels are just some of the neighbors that a squirrel calls his predators. 4. Fairydiddle. 5. If a squirrel makes it through his first year, he is likely to survive for three to five more. In captivity squirrels have lived fifteen to twenty years. **Things you thought you knew about squirrels:** 1. The patagium. 2. No. Flying squirrels have eyes developed for maximum efficiency in low light, but they are unable to see in total darkness. 3. No. Squirrels smell good. In fact, squirrels have a highly developed sense of smell. They use this gift like a French chef, to select only the best cuisine. 4. Squirrels are born naked and blind, but they come into this world with whiskers, claws, and birdseed on the brain. 5. A squirrel needs to eat his own weight in food every week. We know that to be about one pound. The reason some squirrels eat a pound a day is because they can't tell time. **Things you wish you never knew about squirrels:** 1. Duct-tape his mouth shut. 2. Mmm-mmm good. 3. Protein. 4. Yes. A squirrel will adjust his ears frequently to focus on sound. Often he gives the impression that his ears and his eyes are hooked together. 5. No; the sweat glands of a squirrel are in his feet. But get back when he takes his socks off!

"I'm doing a census!"

CHAPTER TWO

The History of Furballs

Squirrel history in a nutshell. In many languages the word for "squirrel" describes the animal—walnut otter, cat in a tree, shadow tail, oak kitten, tail in the air, like a flame, and tree rodent. The gray squirrel, *Sciurus carolinensis*, and the fox squirrel, *Sciurus niger*, are thought to have arrived in North America from the Old World via the ancient land bridge across the Bering Straits. The gray squirrel is often called the cat squirrel because of its catlike call, and the fox squirrel is sometimes called the red squirrel, which always causes confusion because of the larger red squirrel. The fox squirrel probably obtained its name because its color is similar to that of a fox.

Squirrels were once known as migratory animals. Early farmers in North America looked on them as furry locusts coming to devour their crops. In many cases, that is exactly what they did. John Bachman, a naturalist and John James Audubon's collaborator, described this migration:

> Farmers in the western wilds regard them with sensations that may be compared to the anxious apprehensions of the Eastern nations at the flight of the devouring locusts. At such periods, which usually occur in autumn, the squir-

rels congregate in different districts of the far Northwest; and in irregular troops, bend their way instinctively in an eastern direction. Mountains, cleared fields, and narrow bays of some of our lakes, or our broad rivers, present no unconquerable impediment. Onward they come, devouring on the way everything that is suited to their taste, laying waste the corn and wheat fields of the farmer; and as their numbers are thinned by the gun, the dog, and the club, others fall in and fill up the ranks, till they occasion infinite mischief, and call forth more than empty threats of vengeance.

Ordinarily averse to entering the water, they now take to it boldly, and, though swimming with difficulty, manage to cross broad rivers, like the Niagara and Ohio, though many are drowned in the attempt. . . .

Sometimes, when on these migrations, especially after crossing rivers, the squirrels become so fatigued as to be easily captured, and thousands are then killed by boys, armed merely with sticks and stones. I learned from Dr. John A. Kennicott that, during one of these migrations, innumerable squirrels swam across the river Niagara and landed near Buffalo, New York, in such a state of exhaustion that boys caught them in their hands, or knocked them from the fences and bushes with poles.

They swam the Hudson in various places between Waterford and Saratoga; those which we observed crossing the river were swimming deep and awkwardly, their bodies and tails wholly submerged; several that had been drowned were carried downstream, and those which were so fortunate as to reach the opposite bank, were so wet and fatigued, that the boys stationed there with clubs found no difficulty in securing them alive, or in killing them.

The ranks of this impressive squirrel migration were gradually thinned by expanded clearing, increased population, and the dexterity of sportsmen who hunted them for various reasons.

The story goes that one large group of squirrels, forced to migrate by lack of food, headed north out of New York State for Canada. When the mass reached the Niagara River, its members hesitated before attempting to cross the swiftly running water. After a few "I dare ya"s, one after another jumped in and spread their tails as water wings. Most made it ashore a mile or so downstream. (I think once the new free trade legislation begins working better we could share more of our squirrels with our wonderful neighbors to the north. I know I have a couple. I'll even pay the shipping charges and a duty.)

Another story without a date tells of a river crossing by fox squirrels in Pike County, Pennsylvania:

> An immense army of squirrels arrived at the banks of the Delaware River late one night, and commenced its passage by swimming the next morning.
>
> The whole population turned out, and boys and men, equipped with large grain sacks and clubs, killed them by the thousands. They kept coming in a continuous stream throughout the morning, and passed on to the woods beyond. Nothing could deflect them from their course, as they were evidently bound for a fixed point.

Many of these migrations were probably caused by food shortages as well as habitat overcrowding. We solved that for them. We not only reduced their habitat, we reduced the whole species by about 90 percent. The least we can do now is share a little birdseed with them!

Covert squirrel operation—possible CIA involvement. Documents have recently been released by the government that show a covert squirrel operation during the Eisenhower administration. This information has been kept from the American public for over forty years.

President Eisenhower, an avid golfer, had a putting green installed on the White House lawn. It seems that squirrels were wreaking havoc with Ike's putting green while burying their nuts. Using typical army logic, a group of individuals assigned to the White House Army Signal Agency, which was responsible for sound-recording President Eisenhower's public speeches and providing radio and television sound feeds, was given the task of preventing squirrels from leaving divots on the president's green.

Two squirrels taken as live captives in the operation were forced to make distress calls against their will. The army undercover operators felt that these distress calls on tape would frighten the remaining squirrels away when played over the PA system. When the tape was played, dozens of squirrels on or near the putting green froze in their tracks—for about thirty seconds. They then went back to tearing up Ike's green.

In 1955 the federal government trapped squirrels on the White House grounds and in nearby Lafayette Park and shipped them to the country. The public sided with the squirrels. Some citizens even started showing up at the White House with squirrels and releasing them through the fence near Ike's green. It seems that the White House attracts squirrels because of all the nuts there.

In the late 1970s the National Park Service trapped squirrels in Lafayette Park and relocated them. When people in Washington discovered this, they started taking up collections to buy peanuts for the squirrels. Public sentiment soon forced President Carter (the world's most famous peanut farmer) to suspend the trapping. A commission was appointed to study the squirrel problem around the White House. It was discovered that the acreage around the White House did in fact have a higher density of squirrels than any other place on the planet. It also proved that squirrels migrated back to peanut paradise if deported, and that plant damage could be reduced by using hot chili sauce spray.

No other president has had more pets at the White House than Teddy Roosevelt. His bull terrier, Pete, was exiled from the White House after ripping the pants off the French ambassador. The ambassador no sooner got his pants back on when Teddy's pet flying squirrel landed on his shoulder. (Like father, like sons. One night his boys brought a pony named Algonquin into the White House.)

Despite strict security measures, squirrels and an occasional raccoon come and go as they please through the First Lawn, oblivious to affairs of state.

Albino squirrel towns. I used to think there were two towns that used albino squirrels as their fame factors: Marionville, Missouri, and Olney, Illinois. Now I continue to hear of others. Kenton, Tennessee, has a couple hundred white furballs, and residents there claim their squirrels to be the longest established. Like other places boasting albinos, they claim their white squirrels were left by a Gypsy caravan in 1869. I have heard this Gypsy caravan story before, but it was a town farther west. I would think if it were important who the first white squirrel settlers were, all we would have to do is find out which direction those Gypsies were headed.

"I thought all squirrels were white!"

When you drive into Kenton, the first thing you see is a giant billboard across from city hall: "Kenton, Home of the White Squirrels." These white squirrels are also protected by law. Anyone caught killing one is fined $50.

No one seems to know the exact origin of the town's squirrels but it is said that about twenty years ago Jessie Carroll, who was ninety-seven then and as sharp as a tack, told a story of how they got here. Jessie said that when he was a little boy, his father's farm was bordered on one side by a lane from Yorkville to Kenton. Late one afternoon, a Gypsy caravan came down the lane and asked to stay the night.

His father let them stay out in the barn, and the next morning, as a token of their appreciation, the Gypsies wanted to give him something. They walked to the back of the wagon and opened it. Inside was a menagerie of small animals, and among them were two white squirrels. That's how it all started.

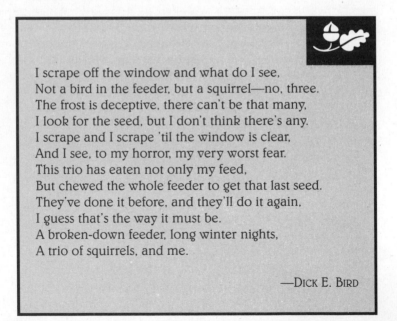

I scrape off the window and what do I see,
Not a bird in the feeder, but a squirrel—no, three.
The frost is deceptive, there can't be that many,
I look for the seed, but I don't think there's any.
I scrape and I scrape 'til the window is clear,
And I see, to my horror, my very worst fear.
This trio has eaten not only my feed,
But chewed the whole feeder to get that last seed.
They've done it before, and they'll do it again,
I guess that's the way it must be.
A broken-down feeder, long winter nights,
A trio of squirrels, and me.

—DICK E. BIRD

Even though the stories of how they got there don't always jibe, most people agree that the first white squirrels probably appeared in Tennessee about 130 years ago.

Olney, Illinois, has the best marketing department of all albino squirrel towns. It calls itself "Home of the White Squirrels." The people there claim that most of the other communities trying to steal their thunder have squirrels with dark eyes, not true albinos. Olney laws give the squirrels right-of-way on every street; residents are fined if they try to leave town with one. The local police patch even bears an outline of a bushy-tailed albino squirrel.

Then there is Marionville, Missouri. These people are bent out of shape because they say their white squirrels arrived just after the Civil War, when they escaped from a traveling circus. Olney has a law against anyone taking a squirrel out of town, but Marionville people claim Olney people kidnapped white squirrels from their town. The squirrels aren't talking, and no one has yet found a stool pigeon. Both towns livetrap and remove common gray squirrels from town.

Normally, white squirrels, which are actually albino gray squirrels, would not survive because of their visibility. In these towns, they thrive because of natural selection by people who have preserved the white squirrels until they now have a significant population. Wildlife experts say that finding any albino animal colony the size of those in the several communities celebrating white squirrel colonies is rare.

Another legend that makes the rounds in these towns has it that two white squirrels escaped from a traveling circus. Another theory is that a weird experiment by a local scientist created the white furballs, and still another claims that a Chinese couple brought them. I think it might have been a local weirdo who became a Chinese scientist and joined the circus with two white squirrels.

White squirrels and white squirrel legends can also be found along the Blue Ridge Mountains. One population belongs to Brevard, North Carolina, where the townspeople even have an ordinance to protect their rare white squirrels. According to one theory, two squirrels, Adam and Eve, came from a traveling carnival—that circus theme again. This carnival happened to travel through Florida. The squirrels escaped and moved into a pecan grove. The grove owner captured the squirrels and gave them to a friend from North Carolina. The friend gave them to his daughter as pets, and she promptly let them escape. This was 1951. By 1986 the Brevard City Council voted unanimously to pass an ordinance protecting them, which states: "The entire area embraced within the corporate limits of the city is hereby designated as a sanctuary for all species of squirrel (family Sciuridae), and in particular the 'Brevard White Squirrel.' It shall be unlawful for any person to hunt, kill, trap, or otherwise take protected squirrels within the city."

Although many of these white squirrel populations seem to come from a circus background, the townspeople who protect them are not clowning around. Stiff fines and even jail time threaten those individuals who would harm one.

Peanut popularity. Military troops in the American Civil War were given peanuts as rations, and in 1865, when soldiers returned to their homes, the previously unknown peanut was suddenly in high demand. With its introduction as a snack food by P. T. Barnum at his circus in 1870, the peanut soon became popular throughout the country. Before long, squirrels were demanding them. Squirrels found peanuts addictive and began hanging out at circuses, which might explain how albino squirrels ended up in towns where circuses visited.

"Home of the Black Squirrels." Marysville, Kansas, bills itself as "The Black Squirrel Town." And the black squirrel is Marysville's official mascot. Every year the town holds the Black Squirrel Celebration. In 1987 the "Black Squirrel Song" became Marysville's official anthem. The city ordinance protects the black squirrels, and one of them is depicted on the official city flag. The black squirrels arrived in

Marysville in the late 1920s, when they escaped from a traveling circus—or was it a Gypsy caravan? It's no mystery how the black squirrels arrived in Hobbs, New Mexico, at least—several were "borrowed" or "stolen" from Marysville in the early 1970s. Hobbs wanted to establish a breeding population in its public parks. The squirrels were turned loose amid much fanfare—and promptly killed by red fox squirrels that Hobbs had imported earlier from Sadler, Texas. Now, all of Hobbs's black squirrels are gone, and Marysville isn't about to lend any more.

I wonder what would happen if we started an exchange student program between Marysville and Kenton, Olney, Marionville, and Brevard. White squirrels could learn to be black, and black squirrels could learn to be white.

National Guarding squirrels. Kent State University is best known for the National Guard's shooting of demonstrators, but it is also famous for its black squirrels. Ten black squirrels were imported from Canada in February 1961 by Larry Woodell, superintendent of grounds. At first, they were mistaken for skunks, but the university quickly added biology courses to the curriculum. Today the black squirrel is the school mascot, and even the English majors can tell the difference between a skunk and a squirrel. The black squirrel on campus is highly regarded and heavily guarded.

World-traveling squirrels. Regardless of its color phase, the gray squirrel has been traced back 30 to 50 million years, when a fossil record was made in North America. It is believed that they were first introduced to North America 50 million years ago by a Gypsy caravan crossing a land bridge from Asia. Gray squirrels were introduced in England as early as 1820, but the majority of the transplants took place in the first two decades of the twentieth century. They started out as royal visitors, being sponsored by the duke of Bedford in the United Kingdom and the earl of Granard in Ireland. Now they have become a royal pain in the posterior. The British complain that American squirrels are overfed, oversexed, and over here—complaints once directed at American GIs during World War II.

Gray squirrels were also introduced into South Africa by Prime Minister Cecil Rhodes in the early 1900s. They have done very well where oak and pine forest is found.

Some grays even became Aussies. A small population was introduced around the vicinity of Melbourne. They did not find the conditions there to their liking and quickly died out. Most species introduced into a foreign habitat will not survive, or do poorly.

The British continue to slander the North American gray squirrel because of current immigration problems. Immigrants brought many species of birds with them when they came to North America. Lucky for us, most of these species did not find conditions suitable for survival here. Two species that have done very well competing for nesting habitat with native species are the starling and the English sparrow. Many people despise these birds and would love to see them deported.

Yanks took their revenge for these introductions—in a way. In 1890 ten gray squirrels were shipped out of New Jersey and given to the duke of Bedford for his estate at Woburn. The squirrels found life very relaxing on the duke's English countryside estate. Before long, the duke had so many furballs, he started giving them to his friends.

At the same time, many other gray squirrels were shipped to Europe as caged pets. Many of these animals chewed their way to freedom and became illegal aliens.

It wasn't long before American squirrels established a bad reputation. The English, Irish, and Scots put a bounty on them and started handing out free cartridges to hunters. This did little to stem the gray squirrel's population explosion.

Battle of the bulging squirrels. "Yankee, go home" is how the European red squirrel feels, in a nutshell, about this intruder. The European red squirrel is not as aggressive and is being driven to extinction by loss of habitat to the Yanks. Other reasons might include disease, competition for food—red squirrels love ripe hazelnuts, but the grays snatch them before they mature—stress, or just not wanting to share real estate with pushy American squirrels. (We can all relate to that.)

Britain's once bountiful red squirrel has been all but dethroned by its more aggressive American gray cousin. But Britain says it can bring back the red squirrel—a shyer, smaller variety that once roamed London's parks in abundance—by shooting and poisoning gray ones, so British conservation officials are killing gray squirrels in areas where red squirrels still live or will be reintroduced.

A new strategy is being launched by the government's Joint Nature Conservation Committee. "Gray squirrels are here to stay in this country," said committee chairman Lord Selborne. "We are not going to exterminate them." Poison, administered through special feeding hoppers designed to be accessible only to grays, would be used only in a few areas.

The English also accuse the North American gray squirrel of completely girdling hardwood trees and killing many of them. They have gone as far as pointing that same accusing finger at Americans and suggesting that we sent them some bark-busting variety we wanted deported instead of the usual nut-loving gray.

We may never learn to leave things as we found them. Upsetting the balance of nature is a very dangerous procedure. The problems created by moving just one species into a niche that was not designed for it are amazingly complex.

I don't think it is possible to work out a trade to resolve this international crisis. First, I am not sure we need any more squirrels on this side of the pond. Second, Europe would not hold all the starlings and English sparrows that have flourished here in the past century.

Queen Elizabeth II has her own personal royal rodent that cleans out her bird feeder every morning. She says she doesn't care because the gardener fills it all the time. I bet when no one is looking she screams at her squirrels and chases them with the garden hose just like the rest of us commoners.

The red squirrel was in control of northern Europe long before the Romans started pushing their weight around. According to an early myth, at the very center of the world grew a mighty ash whose branches reached over all heaven and earth, linking the two worlds. The tree was constantly threatened by its inhabitants, which included an eagle, whose flapping wings caused the wind, and a great serpent, along with myriad other smaller snakes, who gnawed at its base. These opposing forces were linked by a squirrel, Ratatosk, who ran up and down the trunk, carrying insults back and forth between the eagle and snakes.

Red squirrels were also holy to the Teutonic thunder god Donar, the predecessor of Thor. Donar was closely associated with the great oaks of the forests, and—perhaps since he was described as having red hair, a red beard, and "beetling red eyebrows"—the similarly colored red squirrel acquired special significance. To this day, the red squirrel remains a favorite character in folk stories and fairy tales throughout Europe. How will parents explain to their children that Beatrix Potter's Squirrel Nutkin is extinct?

In little more than a century, imported-from-America gray squirrels have toppled British red squirrels from their perches of privilege. The British are now ready to fight back. Hopefully, it's not too late to save Squirrel Nutkin's red kins' skin.

- Gray squirrels appear to be better adapted to the current fragmented British woodland. They had plenty of practice here after we clear-cut most of North America's timber.
- The shy, red *Sciurus vulgaris*, which ranges widely across continental Europe, is slender, has tufted ears, weighs about ten ounces, and spends most of its time in trees.
- The gray intruder is *Sciurus carolinensis*. It is plump with

short ears, weighs up to one and a half pounds, is an inch or two longer than the reds, and is often seen on the ground.
- Reds are happiest in conifers, eating cones and seeds high off the ground. They cannot easily digest acorns.
- The grays are less discriminating feeders. They love acorns and are happier than a corn borer in a peach among deciduous hardwoods, which make up the vast majority of woodlands in England.

Not only do the grays outcompete the reds, but there is also a suspicion that they may carry a virus that does not affect them but can infect other squirrels. Although red squirrels are a protected species under British law, conservationists believe that passive defense cannot save them. The reds are now the most widely spread squirrel species in the world, but perhaps not for long.

Logging camp squirrels. It is ironic that so many lumbering terms are based on squirrels and their habits, since the practice of clear-cutting timber that has devastated much of North America's forests at one time pushed squirrels to the brink of extinction in many ranges.

A **squirrel** is a counterweight to pull a loading boom into position where only one swing line is used. Often the squirrel is a short chunk of log that rides up and down the spar, just like a squirrel on a tree. It is also used in places to pull slack on the tong line to make it easier for the loaders.

A **squirrel line** is a light line used for many odd jobs around a logging camp.

A **squirrel tree** is one so full of branches that it is good for nothing but squirrel perches.

A **squirrel man** is a high-climbing logger.

Paul Bunyan had a squirrel named Lefty in his Michigan lumber camp who was hit by a falling timber and was never right again. Some say Lefty was a mudslinger, but no one ever proved it. This species is believed extinct, but before the northern forests were clear-cut they were quite abundant, even though not one was ever seen. Mudslingers ate a lot more birds than other species of squirrel. They would sneak through the underbrush raising and lowering themselves to look for prey. Upon spying something tasty, a mudslinger squirrel would tilt itself back on its tail, using its feet to create a tripod firing stance. It would then let fly a pellet of regurgitated mud and feathers. Just like the big league pitchers, these squirrels kept an ample supply of material in their cheeks at all times.

"I bought all new walnut furniture for the den, dear!"

Because of all the clear-cutting, these squirrels would never pass up opportunities to fire mudballs at a crew of lumberjacks. These squirrels were so accurate that they could pick out the straw boss at a hundred feet and paste him when he had his back to his crew. The straw boss never believed in mudslingers and always blamed the dirt ball on some poor laborer who was just trying to make an honest buck.

The fact that not one of these squirrels was ever spotted does not mean they did not exist. It is believed that the mudslinger's territory must have stretched all the way across the country because rail builders also encountered them. Some old-timers swore they saw mudslingers in action. They say these critters didn't stand in a tripod position and they weren't squirrels. They said that laborers only made a small amount of money for a large amount of work, the straw bosses were taskmasters, and the work was boring. The mudslinger was invented to help pass the time and entertain the troops. The laborers would all get together and place bets on who could clobber the boss at the greatest distance. Sometimes the pot would grow for days before someone connected. The boss could never pin the deed on anyone because the men all stuck together with the mudslinger story.

So what's so far-fetched about a tripod mudslinging squirrel? Mother Nature has certainly played worse tricks on herself. Take man, for example. It might make life more interesting if squirrels could shoot back!

Famous show-biz squirrel. As with Lassie, there have been several Twiggys. This famous water-skiing squirrel has worked the outdoor and boat show circuit for years, performing her amazing water skills on skis. There were two predecessors of the current Twiggy. The first started her entertainment career in 1978. She had a long and successful headlining act for nine years. Two other squirrels continue the water-skiing gig under the name Twiggy. In late 1997 the owner of Twiggy, Chuck Best, passed away, but squirrels are still skiing. Squirrels are natural entertainers. Boat shows or backyards—it makes absolutely no difference to them. They just want the spotlight.

Some people will do anything to watch squirrels entertain. An accountant from Munich turned to crime to fuel his addiction to feeding and watching squirrels. Herman Arseberg, thirty four, was so taken in by the "gentle, trusting" squirrels, when he first fed them hazelnuts in his local park, that he began skipping work to visit them. He then began fiddling his firm's books to buy extra nuts. He was finally arrested driving through the Black Forest in a van with eight tons of nuts in the back. The worst side to this tragic story is—the squirrels were just using him. They didn't love him; they were just being nice so that he would bring them nuts. They all knew he was cooking the books to feed them, but they just didn't care.

Review and Relate

- Squirrels have a wonderful family tree. In ancient times they were known as the "fire animal." The Native Americans believed that squirrels brought fire to the earth for the benefit of man.
- A squirrel's life span in the wild is somewhere between two and six years. But if you are friendly with your squirrels and share birdseed, they can live at your bird feeder for up to fifteen years.
- A squirrel has four toes on his front feet and five on his back feet.
- Squirrels use urine to mark their territories. They will also leave scent trails using oil and sweat glands.
- A female squirrel with a life span of twelve years can easily raise sixty or more offspring.
- Squirrels will slowly molt and change their coats twice a year. The important tail and ear coverings will usually molt just once a year.
- It is believed that squirrels have a social hierarchy determined by physical stature. They use their tails to measure each other. The longer the reach, the more food a squirrel can paw out of a squirrel-proof feeder. The more food a squirrel can steal, the higher his social status.
- Squirrels have whiskers on the sides of their noses and around the eyes. These long feelers give them sensory skills they use in low-light situations, such as inside a windowless metal squirrel-proof bird feeder.
- Gray squirrels commonly occur in two color phases, gray and black. This leads many people to believe that they're two different species.
- The true meaning of the Latin word for squirrel, *sciurus,* is derived from two Greek words, *skia,* meaning shadow, and *oura,* meaning tail. If you combine the words, it means that the squirrel carries his patio cabana with him wherever he goes.
- A squirrel can lose part of his tail to a predator and still survive.

- During the winter, small holes in the snow or ground around the yard indicate that squirrels have been digging for dinner. Their caches may contain acorns, hickory nuts, pecans, beechnuts, pine seeds, butternuts, walnuts, or that fifty-pound bag of black oil sunflower seed that is missing from the garage.
- Squirrels will often swim across large bodies of water to reach food sources. Crossing lakes or rivers, a number of squirrels will be preyed upon by large freshwater fish, like walleye and especially northern pike. Maybe that is why fishing-lure companies buy so many squirrel tails from hunters.
- There are legends of migrating squirrels crossing rivers by dragging pieces of bark to the water, jumping aboard, and floating to the other side. (Those were just the ones that didn't want to get their feet wet.) In mass migration, it was not unusual for squirrels to swim rivers in large numbers.
- A squirrel once shut down NASDAQ's computer center in Trumbull, Connecticut. No one lost his life savings, but the squirrel did lose his life. It was another case of senseless electrocution. The squirrel was short in a bull market.
- If you want squirrel-proof bird feeders, it is going to take imagination. Don't confuse an imagination with an inventive mind. Nothing is squirrel-proof, so you need to spend a lot of time pretending there is.
- Thinking you are smarter than a squirrel feels just as good as being smarter than a squirrel—if you are convincing enough to fool yourself.

- A New York bank decided to use the squirrel as an example of a poor saver. The bank ran ads showing a confused squirrel trying to remember where he buried his nuts. It wasn't long before the mailbag was full of letters from customers defending the squirrel and his habits. Feelings were so strong that the ad campaign was dropped, and an apology was issued.

• In the early 1800s, squirrels migrating from area to area in the fall of the year traveled in gatherings estimated to contain nearly a quarter million individuals. There are records, not to be disputed, of bands of squirrels advancing along fronts a hundred miles wide and requiring five days to pass. (And you think you have problems!)

• There are legends of squirrels in migration crossing rivers by dragging pieces of bark to the water, jumping aboard, and floating to the other side. Those without bark canoes did the dog-paddle.

• In the early days of the space program, when we were sending up our first experimental rockets, NASA wanted to send a squirrel into space instead of a monkey. This never happened because after a long search, officials could not find a squirrel with the right stuff.

• One early campaign to wipe out nuisance squirrels in 1749 eliminated 640,000 squirrels in Pennsylvania in one year. This bounty system cost the colony treasury eight thousand pounds sterling.

• When George Bush moved into the White House, he said, "Squirrels on the White House lawn are history." He figured his dog Millie would chase them all away. What actually took place was a peace accord. Millie agreed not to chase squirrels if they wouldn't tell anyone what she was doing to the rosebushes.

• Thomas Seton estimated that nearly half a billion squirrels took part in the 1842 emigration that passed through Wisconsin, heading southwest. It lasted for weeks. This was an army of squirrels a hundred and thirty miles wide and one hundred and fifty miles long. By 1900 conservationists feared that the eastern gray squirrel might become extinct.

• In 1808, Ohio required each free white man to deliver 100 squirrel scalps a year or pay a $3 fine.

• John James Audubon was so fascinated by the squirrel's wanderlust that he gave the name "migrating squirrel," or *Sciurus migratorius,* to what he thought was a separate species but turned out to be just another gray squirrel.

- A hundred years ago squirrels would migrate through vast areas of the North American forests in huge numbers, searching for good seed and nut crops. The squirrels of today are relatively sedentary, spending their five- to six-year life spans on your bird feeder.
- A squirrel skull exhibits greater width between the eye sockets and depth through the cranium than any other rodent. This large brain cavity does not necessarily make a squirrel smarter; as any squirrel will tell you, "It's not what ya got, it's how you use it."
- Squirrels think globally and act locally.
- A squirrel is a very lucky animal. This could be because he is always carrying an acorn. People have believed for thousands of years that carrying an acorn protects against disease and ensures long life.
- Researchers estimate that only one gray squirrel in 10,000 is black phase. This mutant resides primarily in northern climates. Biologists theorize that the black fur more readily absorbs the warmth of the sun, thereby keeping the squirrel warmer during cold winters and giving it a survival advantage.

Scientists have uncovered what they believe to be the world's oldest squirrel skull. They believe the cause of death may have been a severe blow to the skull, perhaps from a

expandable cheekbone   **where the rock landed**

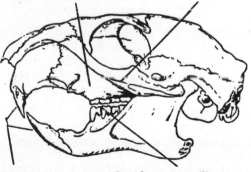

seed incisors   **molariform sunflower crushers**

rock. Petroglyphs found on cave walls near the find draw researchers to the conclusion that this specimen may have been in a gourd tray of seed cave dwellers had placed out to attract songbirds. One crude drawing shows a loincloth-clad cave dweller chasing a squirrel with a stick.

Tree Rat Trivia

THINGS YOU SHOULD KNOW ABOUT SQUIRRELS

1. How does a gray squirrel move her young?
2. Is a squirrel double-jointed?
3. How big is a squirrel's brain?
4. How are squirrels used to describe alert humans?
5. How many nests will a squirrel have?

THINGS YOU THOUGHT YOU KNEW ABOUT SQUIRRELS

1. What do you do if a squirrel moves into your attic?
2. Where should you relocate a squirrel to ensure he won't return?
3. How do you keep a squirrel from digging?
4. What did the Chippewa Indian name for "squirrel" mean?
5. How far can a squirrel jump?

THINGS YOU WISH YOU NEVER KNEW ABOUT SQUIRRELS

1. What is the best way to keep a squirrel from eating your birdseed?
2. What is the most irritating thing about a squirrel?
3. What mammal is the red squirrel's most serious predatory threat?
4. What is the most widely spread squirrel species in the world?
5. What do taxidermists call a squirrel tail that is twelve inches long?

Trivia Answers

Things you should know about squirrels: 1. She seizes one young squirrel at a time by the soft, stretchy skin on its belly. The youngster then curls its body around either side of the mother's head and is carried that way. 2. Yes—not only do they live in two different types of nest, but squirrels have long, muscular hind legs and short front legs for leaping. To help the squirrel scurry headfirst up and down tree trunks, the hind legs are double-jointed. 3. A squirrel's brain is about the size of a walnut because that is all he has thought about for the past 50 million years. 4. "Bright-eyed and bushy-tailed." 5. It depends on how many fleas a squirrel has. When one nest or den becomes infested, a squirrel will move and leave no forwarding address. **Things you thought you knew about squirrels:** 1. Make him sign a long-term lease with an option to buy. 2. Find a nice yard at least three miles from your home with lots of bird feeders. 3. Lock the shovel in the garage. 4. The Chippewa Indian recognized the peculiar habit of the squirrel using his tail for shade in the name he gave to the squirrel, which translates to "tail in the air." 5. With enough height, a good tailwind, and enough sunflower seed as the prize—about a quarter mile. On average, in normal conditions, about eight to ten feet. **Things you wish you never knew about squirrels:** 1. Duct-tape his mouth shut. 2. He chews with his mouth open. 3. The most threatening natural enemy of the red squirrel is the pine marten. 4. The Eurasian red squirrel, commonly found throughout Europe and northern Asia. 5. A foot.

*Birds
Are from
Saturn*

*Squirrels
Are from
Uranus*

CHAPTER THREE

The Practical Solution of Squirrel-Feeding in Your Backyard

Now that we've got the nuts and bolts on our squirrels, let's take a look at how they interact with our backyard birds.

Feed 'em and breed 'em. I spent many years in the bird-feeder manufacturing business. In all those years, no one ever told me a bird story—I was always told squirrel stories. Most of the stories were about the amazing acrobatic abilities that squirrels possess or one of the many ways to thwart them. There were those people who loved to hate their squirrels and those who loved to love their squirrels. I always felt there was a huge consumer population that enjoyed feeding squirrels as much as the songbirds that visit their yards.

Let's look at this from a historic point of view. At one time squirrels owned this country. They could travel from the Atlantic to the Mississippi, tree to tree, without ever touching the ground, except to cross a few rivers. Oh yes, squirrels can swim. They do the dog-paddle and use their tails as rudders. They do not swim as a recreational hobby, but they will if they have to, especially if food is involved.

A couple hundred years ago, people started showing up on the eastern seaboard and clear-cutting the continent. At first the squirrels were a little upset. But they soon discovered that the trees were being replaced with corn—fields of dreams. Obviously, the squirrels were thinking the corn was for them—I mean, the trees were theirs! But soon the war broke out. I don't mean the Revolutionary War, I mean the great squirrel war. There were millions of squirrels, and they were all addicted to corn. The lead started flying. Lead, at the time, was a rare commodity, so farmers would "bark" squirrels. If he shot the squirrel with his black powder rifle, chances are he would never find his lead ball. The trick was to shoot the bark of the tree close enough to the squirrel or squirrels so the flying bark would kill or wound them. Oftentimes a farmer could get two or more squirrels if he were lucky. The farmer would then collect his squirrels and dig his lead ball out of the tree to remelt and re-form.

Keeping squirrels from eating precious crops turned out to be a decades-long cold war. The Industrial Revolution was, in the end, good for the squirrel. It created a new lifestyle for millions of workers. Town fringes turned into suburban communities. Leisure time allowed landscaping and gardening and feeding birds. The first few decades of bird feeding created a lot of animosity toward squirrels who would dare to help themselves to birdseed left out for the birds. Efforts to curb their appetite for birdseed failed; squirrels refused to give in to strong-arm tactics and continued to take everything they could get away with. A majority of people have quit trying to outflank their furballs and instead just give them what they want. To save face, many of these people pretend they like the squirrels in their yards.

What goes around comes around. For whatever reasons, near the end of the twentieth century, hundreds of farmers in North America make their living growing corn and sunflower seed for the sole purpose of feeding squirrels. Squirrel feeding has become a multimillion-dollar sub-industry of the multibillion-dollar bird-feeding industry. Even Rubbermaid, which never made a wood product in its previous business history, now makes an aromatic cedar squirrel feeder.

But this doesn't mean you have to follow the crowd and give up on trying to outwit the squirrels that cause you the most stress. Many productive people are happy today only because they have been able to fill the void left in their lives since retirement by occupying their days and evenings figuring out ways to keep squirrels off their bird feeders. These are the people who keep the patent office in business. After people convince themselves that their antisquirrel contraptions or methods work, they patent them and try to convince you. If there is any doubt in your mind that nothing is squirrel-proof, check out *Daylight Thieves I & II* on the Discovery Channel, a film put together by the British Broadcasting Corporation. The film starts out with a squirrel at a bird feeder. Then there is an attempt to baffle the squirrel using various hardware. Once the squirrel figures out and circumvents one baffle, another is added. By the end of the film, the starring squirrel gets through the whole gauntlet of baffles in under thirty seconds. The last obstacle is a three-foot jump into a small-diameter plastic tube. In the tube is a toy wagon. After successfully entering the tube, the squirrel had to lie on the wagon and belly-crawl it through the tube.

THE GREAT SQUIRLINDAS

Coming soon to a yard near you! Working high above the ground without a net, this act is hard to follow. They will be performing the death-defying pyramid feeder fall, where the whole group hits the feeder at one time and juggles large striped sunflower seeds. As a grand finale they will make the entire contents of the feeder disappear before your very eyes. Don't miss these amazing acrobats.

The squirrel in this film, a female North American gray squirrel, should be very familiar to you, and not just because of her skill level: at the very end of the film, they pan a tree and show a copy of my Hairy Houdini "Squirrel Wanted" poster. Even though I invented the poster as a spoof on squirrel prejudice, prejudice is very much the case in Europe. Many people think that our black squirrels were introduced here from Britain. Not so (our black squirrels are only one of the many color phases of gray squirrel); it is the other way around—our gray squirrel was introduced in Europe, and has done very well for itself across the pond. In Britain the gray squirrel is being annihilated because it is driving the European red squirrel to extinction. This should make all the people on this side of the pond who hate the European starling and the English sparrow feel as if they have retaliated. Tit for tat, two birds for a rat.

Food co-op. Sharing food is never voluntary for most wild animals. Mice will dig up nuts buried by squirrels and chipmunks; blue jays will rip off mushrooms that squirrels leave to dry on branches. When a squirrel finds he has been had, he can be heard. It is often just a verbal battle or may be a good chase scene. In most cases no one is injured unless the chasee or the chaser does not look both ways before crossing the roadee and gets flattened by the roadster. Food is not considered property to most animals in the same sense that a nest or territory is defended. Squirrels do not eat to live, but live to eat. Take a squirrel to lunch!

Birds are from Saturn, squirrels are from Uranus. Squirrels have somehow come to think of themselves as Rulers of the World. Birds, on the other hand, have a much more subtle lifestyle and are symbolic of happiness and virtue. To the Romans, Saturn was considered the god of agriculture and vegetation. This is very fitting, since birds are responsible for much of our planet's seed dispersal, pollination, and fertilization.

Songbirds and squirrels do not harmonize well together, but that does not mean they cannot coexist. Sharing does not always have to include caring. A lack of love can be overcome with proper logistics. Songbirds learn not to dine around furballs. Timing is everything. Never having to say "I love you" is a squirrel's way of life.

The relationship between squirrels and birds at the feeder can be very political. There is a species bias and/or confusion about who has the most admiration and love for black oil sunflower seed. Squirrels want to be praised for their strength in the face of difficulty and admired for how well they are coping, learning, and taking control of a difficult bird-feeding situation. Birds, on the other hand, just want to eat and not be eaten, flit and not be flustered, nest and not be noticed.

Even when having the same thoughts, birds express themselves one way and squirrels another. The biggest difference between the species is that birds will admit to not knowing how to get the last little seed out of a tight tube feeder, while squirrels will consistently come up with a solution. In an impossible seed situation a bird will say, "I don't get it." In the same situation a squirrel will quite literally gnaw on the problem until he finds the answer.

A squirrel's need is to feel successful in a baffled situation. A bird's basic need is to be fulfilled and full at all times. A bird wants to feel part of a relationship, and a squirrel would rather just eat alone.

Uranusians and Saturnarians can occupy the same space, but seldom at the same time. A Saturnarian bird must give a Uranusian squirrel some space. If not, the squirrel will tend to take it. It's a get-close, back-off relationship. Uranusians have this "I'm okay, you're not okay" mentality.

Squirrels are jumpy; birds are flighty. Most squirrels are

Hey, you guys, get off that feeder.
It's not for furballs, it's for tweeters.
If I catch you there again,
I'll make you wish you'd never been.
I'm planning your impending doom,
I'll send my wife out with the broom.

—DICK E. BIRD

authoritarians; most birds are vegetarians. Birds and squirrels would communicate and relate better by acknowledging their differences, but they won't.

At one time Saturnians and Uranusians respected and accepted their differences and their desires for the same seed. Then they came to your backyard and forgot they were from different parts of the canopy.

Squirrels are what they eat. Just what is it that squirrels prefer to eat? Historically, they are responsible for planting most of the oak trees in North America. They accomplished this by gathering and burying nuts every season and then forgetting where they put most of them. Scientists call this "rodent retention deficit." Perhaps squirrels are not so forgetful. Does it not make sense that if they planted more oaks, they would harvest more acorns? It is my contention that squirrels are better timber managers than those currently in charge at local, state, and federal levels.

Actually, as we've seen, a squirrel will eat anything that doesn't eat him first. In general, squirrels like mushrooms, nuts, seeds, bird eggs, fruits, and vegetables. They do not have a clue that you are putting goodies out for your birds. Not only do they think you are putting birdseed out for them, they also believe you are putting out hummingbird nectar, orange halves, peanut butter, suet, bread crumbs, and all the other delicacies you have in mind for your birds for them too. One thing you can't label a squirrel as is "picky eater."

Many people have tried to convince me over the years that if you put out some form of inexpensive feed, like cracked corn, and locate it a long way from the bird feeders, squirrels will concentrate on the corn and stay out of the more expensive sunflower seed. If you believe this, you are probably also waiting at the door for Ed and Dick to show up with your sweepstakes check. Most squirrels are born at night, but it wasn't last night! If you are offering sunflower seed, it will definitely have an effect on squirrel migration through your yard. If you don't believe me, try this: Next time you have a party, offer a dish of crackers without spread in one corner of the room and another dish of crackers spread with Philadelphia strawberry cream cheese in another corner. I guarantee that within a minute the topic of conversation will be carried out by your guests in a touch-and-go flight pattern around the crackers with the cream cheese. To a squirrel, sunflower seeds are equivalent to Philadelphia strawberry cream cheese on crackers.

Sadistic safflower seed. Some miserable soul came up with the idea that squirrels didn't care for safflower seed. Obviously, this character has never had the pleasure of meeting Hairy Houdini, who loves the stuff. But a majority of the squirrel kingdom does find the flavor and texture of safflower seed unappetizing, especially if they have other delicacies readily available. But before you run out and buy a fifty-pound bag of safflower seed, consider this: A majority of birds thinks the stuff stinks too! So here's what you end up with: a select group of songbirds, like the beautiful cardinal, that loves safflower seed, and a bunch of low-life squirrels that will eat anything that starts with F, ends with D, and has a couple O's in the middle.

All you have done by offering safflower seed is lose your classier squirrel clientele and a great number of bird species. If you haven't figured it out yet—squirrels are opportunists. They have very small gears in their brains that are in continual motion. They are not brilliant; they are just constant thinkers. They are successful for the same reason the tortoise always beats the hare. They do not chew your feeders to punish you for sometimes being less than hospitable. They chew on feeders and decks and siding and electrical wires because their teeth grow like fingernails. If they didn't chew on something, they would end up with severe overbite, making it impossible for them to chew you out.

Habitat for humility. Squirrels can be very humble, but they like to rumble. You will see them chasing each other through the tree branches, screaming their fool heads off.

This could be love, a territorial dispute, or nature's way of a quick-and-easy divorce. The female ends up with the kids and the house; the male ends up eating out a lot at your bird feeder.

Because a squirrel is so persistent about filling his belly with adequate daily rations, many people think of him as pushy, arrogant, and full of himself. If you get to know your squirrel, you will find him modest, almost meek, in his quest for thrift and organization.

Nothing is cuter than a squirrel with his jowls so full of food that his eyes are forced open. Ninety percent of that cheek stash ends up in a squirrel cache. Squirrels are one of nature's true early-retirement planners. They do not hibernate during the winter, but they do take a lot of time to relax and enjoy life. On cold, blustery days they lie in their dens or dreys and snack away at their stores.

An important safety consideration around the house is squirrel habitat. If you have an abundance of furball neighbors and not a lot of natural habitat, where do you think your squirrelly neighbors are going to start looking for warm, cozy winter quarters? If you don't like them eating your bird feed, just wait until they show up at the dining room table.

If you have an abundant population of squirrels, you most likely have adequate habitat to support their numbers. However, constant pressure from development forces wildlife into smaller and smaller niches. Around your home squirrels will look for real estate that offers them safety, warmth, and a food source. If they can't find that in a tree cavity, leaf nest site, or tree crotch, they may start window-shopping.

Squirrelly neighbors. You can avoid squirrels showing up at your dining room table by offering adequate housing in the general vicinity of your yard. Squirrel houses are as fun to build as birdhouses, and they get used more often *(see page 124)*. You can make it very comfortable for your squirrel if you build a few boxes close together. He will use some of them for storage. In the fall some of my birdhouses are chock-full of dried mushrooms cached by resident squirrels.

Offering squirrels a place to store food for the winter is more of a suggestion than a directive. The easiest way would be to leave a nesting box closed up for the winter if you notice a squirrel using it for a warehouse. Afraid of being robbed, they tend to find dry, secure niches that other nearby squirrels may not think about. Nothing is more frustrating than gathering grub all season and having your cache crashed. This often causes serious problems if homeowners are not cautious. I have had squirrels spend the winter on the engine block of my motor home, lining their den with my carpet and chewing my electrical wiring.

"Some Japanese character said American squirrels are fat and lazy and can't find their own food. I think he's just plain jealous!"

A neighbor lost his milk barn thanks to a furball. A squirrel filled his electrical box with walnuts, causing a short and sparking a fire. Enticing them to stay outside with a little nesting box bait is a lot easier than rewiring and rebuilding.

Never go to bed with a squirrel. They do not make very good bed partners. A lady in Charlotte, North Carolina, had to evict several squirrels from her house. She pulled back her bedcovers one night and found a cache of cashews. When she reached for them, one of her squirrelly neighbors jumped out of bed and latched on to her as if she were a tree branch. He didn't bite. He was just curious about who was stealing his nuts.

The woman almost had a coronary. She went nuts, the nuts went flying, the squirrel went nuts flying after his cache of cashews, and before it was all over the cops were called in to settle the dispute.

Another inexpensive way to keep your squirrels happy, healthy, and—more importantly—busy is to provide some fruit and berry plants for them. This goes hand in hand with offering plant species that attract songbirds. Just about any plant that offers food and cover to your birds will offer the same amenities to your squirrels.

Anchoring your offering. You won't have to worry about squirrels' carrying off your bushes, but everything else you put out is up for grabs. Whether you are trying to feed birds, squirrels, or any other critters that tend to show up when free food is available, you have to anchor your offerings. Squirrels are more afraid of something else getting them than you are of your squirrels getting them. A perfect example of this is one of the latest so-called squirrel-proof bird feeders on the market. This feeder has a nine-volt battery that generates a trickle charge to the feeder's perches. It doesn't affect the birds because they are not grounded. It does, however, give a foraging squirrel a little poke when he tries to perch and poach. I asked a gentleman who bought one of these very expensive devices how he liked it and asked if it was thwarting the squirrels for him. He said that within two days his dominant squirrel not only learned to switch the power off before he ate but switched it back on when he left so no one else would help himself.

The reason that all the cute little table-and-chair squirrel feeders have large spikes securely attached to them is because squirrels seem to enjoy takeout more than eating in. If they have the option, they will take a food offering. They much prefer cache and carry—or is it carry, cache, and bury? Either way, they will steal you blind if you don't open your eyes to the fact that greed is a creed for a squirrel in need.

Now, there is anchoring and creative anchoring. Many people enjoy the latter. It is part of the entertainment value of feeding backyard wildlife. Creative anchoring consists of anything that might challenge or frustrate a squirrel. One example would be to twist a screw eye into an ear of corn and then suspend it using rubber bands. The squirrel reaches out to lean against and attempt to munch on the corn, and he and the corn stretch to their limits. The squirrel will never let go. It is against the law of squirrel nature to release a food source once it is within his grasp.

Another creative way to frustrate your squirrel is the "Olé" method. This is a bit more time-consuming but very rewarding. You find a bird feeder that is very appealing to a squirrel, which of course is *any* bird feeder. You fill it with the best seed money can buy and locate it just outside your window with a convenient squirrel launching pad nearby, such as a fence or a tree. Attach a cord to the bottom of the feeder and run it into the house. When it is all rigged properly, you sit and wait. Do not get trigger-happy: timing is everything. A squirrel will position himself on the launching pad, and you have to watch his eyes. His feet will shake a little, his tail will quiver, but you can always tell by the eyes when he's going to jump. Wait until he has fully deployed before you pull on the cord. This is very perplexing to even the craftiest furballs. They get so frustrated, they talk to themselves. If you do this long enough, you will notice that the squirrel eventually begins to compensate and leads the feeder in anticipation of its movement.

Squirrel factoring. You don't have to be a rocket scientist to feed birds, but an engineering background is a must. Thousands of man-hours are spent annually in the hope that one day there will be a cure for the common squirrel. Secreted away in garages and basements all over North America, gadget gurus are building and testing what might someday turn out to be an honest-to-goodness squirrel-proof bird feeder. Where most fail at this endeavor is by not calculating the "squirrel factor." To foil a furball one must somehow create a marriage between machining and method. Many seemingly great contraptions to outwit the squirrel fall short simply because the squirrel develops methods to circumvent the mechanisms. No other mammal has the acute engineering thought process that the squirrel uses so cunningly.

Squirrel-baffle manufacturers are continually bewildered by the unique methods that squirrels develop to render their products obsolete. An example of this evolutionary process would begin with the Hylarious bird feeder, the first in a series of weight-activated perch feeders that challenged the world of squirrels. The way it worked seemed ingenious enough. The seed was held in a large strongbox-like metal container. On the perch side of the feeder was a long opening that allowed access to the seed. The perch, however, was attached to hinged, weighted arms and a hatch that would shut off access to the seed. The weights could be moved along the arms to determine the exact weight that would force the perch down and close off the seed opening.

This feeder, like all the others, assumed that squirrels are stupid. And since 50 percent of the squirrel population *is* stupid, this feeder worked half the time. Another problem with the design was that one squirrel or ten chickadees could shut the hatch. It wasn't long before people started reporting that one squirrel would sit on the weight while the other ate, and then they would switch. It was squirrel teamwork that sent engineers back to the drawing boards.

The next improvement to this design turned out to be very inventive. Instead of weights, squirrelly engineers made the perch spring-activated. A series of springs beneath the feeder could be adjusted to vary the weight that would close the seed outlet. But it wasn't long before people started complaining that the squirrels were jumping straight into the feeder without ever touching the weight-activated perch.

This made the squirrels very happy. They were high and dry, sitting on a week's worth of groceries, and no one could see them. One lady happened to see a squirrel jump into her feeder. She went out with her husband's nine iron and not only rang that squirrel's bell but also destroyed a $70 feeder.

So, back to the drawing board. With a little more rodent research in hand, engineers designed a half-moon series of baffles that fit into the seed outlet so that seed could flow out but squirrels could not jump in. This would have worked—if not for the squirrel factor. Soon people were complaining that squirrels would climb to the top of the feeder, hang from the claws on their rear feet, stretch their bodies all the way across the top of the feeder, hang with their heads upside down, and fill their faces with seed.

I have often said that you do not have to be a rocket scientist to deal with squirrels, but I do know a retired rocket scientist who once told me he had a solution to the problem of squirrels getting into these perch-activated feeders. First, he tried a piece of plywood on top of the feeder with a dowel going down to the perch. If a squirrel climbed onto the plywood, his weight would force the dowel down and shut off the seed access. This was like having a weight-activated system protecting a weight-activated system. The problem was that snow would also shut it down. He then improved the design with framed hardware cloth. This allowed the snow to pass through but not the squirrel. It was not long after that that he finally confessed to me that the squirrel was now wrapped around the side of the feeder, again filling his face.

Part of the practical solution to squirrel feeding is to admit your limitations when it comes to matching wits with two pounds of muscle, blood, bone, and gray matter.

Hypothesizing squirrel skill. Most squirrel-prevention methods that people try to convince themselves work are not well supported by evidence. In most cases this is called marketing. There is no consumer-protection law that says manufacturers cannot claim squirrel-proofness without data to back it up. Everything they say is conditional. They assume you have only stupid squirrels in your yard. Unfortunately, this is where the highly probable turns out to be a poor assumption. You would be better off both in time and money to just feed and breed your squirrels rather than spending your children's inheritance trying to outfox them.

Squirrel etiquette. You must make up your own mind about how you are going to treat your squirrels. Some decide their squirrels are workaholics, while others decide they are seedaholics. It depends on the squirrel. Some just want food, and others are after the glory. Squirrels never rest on their laurels; they know there will always be another young bird-feeder engineer trying to make a name for himself. Squirrels have busted the best contraptions over the years, but the ideas never stop in attempts to foil and fool. In the spirit of evolution, every spring, squirrels pass out designer genes that continue to guarantee that the future will hold an abundance of crafty critters. Whether you politely invite your squirrels to dine or not, plan on extra place settings.

Aggravated assault. Squirrels tend to do things that make people a little nuts, especially gardeners. Many gardeners love to feed birds. When a squirrel finds a bird-feeding gardener, his fur starts to tingle. This is like squirrel utopia—not only seed, but salad.

While you can't stop a squirrel from digging up your bulbs and eating your harvest, you can attempt to slow him down. Bury hardware cloth in the garden and flowerpots to discourage major squirrel excavation. You can also buy a product that is basically fox urine to spray around the garden. Or better yet, get a fox and give him plenty of water.

"Sure beats playing in the dark!"

Controlling squirrels can turn into a full-time job if you become obsessed. A lady wrote me from British Columbia about a feisty little red squirrel that seemed to dominate her yard. She named him "Vicious" because he would fight with and chase off every other squirrel or bird that tried to come into the woman's bird-feeder sanctuary. Her question was not so much, "What should I do about Vicious?" but rather, "How often will he breed?" She had heard that squirrels will often have two litters per year and was worried that she might have a bunch of little sons of Vicious, strong-arming every critter in her area. She had a legitimate concern; that is exactly what squirrels will do, given an adequate food source. If weather conditions and food availability are favorable, spring and late summer will find three to five blind and naked baby squirrels nestled with their mother. Young squirrels remain in the nest for up to eight weeks while they go through basic training.

Your squirrels may not act according to what you have read. There is a very good explanation for this—squirrels have never read the books. They are supposed to be lounging around all afternoon, but you find them at the feeder from daylight to dusk. They are not supposed to like safflower seed, but you find their cheeks bulging with the stuff. They are supposed to be gun-shy, but you find yours staring you down.

It is not wise to try to categorize your squirrels. Every rascal is not a thief, even though every thief is a rascal. If you are trying to figure out if your squirrel is a rascal or a thief, try spending some time observing him. See if he looks honorable. There is honor among thieves. If your squirrel doesn't look honorable, you most likely have a little rascal on your hands. If you get to know your squirrels in the same appreciative way you have come to know your songbirds, the inventory shrinkage at the feeder will be a lot easier to live with. The backyard café would be a pretty dull place without a few squirrel brawls once in a while to keep things lively.

This is not to say you should let down your guard. You have every right—in fact, it's your duty—to keep that squirrel off your bird feeder. If you didn't try, your furball would be disappointed. He looks forward to the challenge. Getting around a good air defense system, like a squirrel dome, is a daily goal for every squirrel worth his unsalted peanuts.

"I saw the broom—I just thought he wanted to clean the feeder!"

Squirrel protection. Squirrels are protected by local, state, and federal game laws. This means it is illegal for you to take the law into your own hands when you get frustrated with certain individuals in your yard. Some states are more specific. California, for instance, has Penal Code 6260, which is part of the State Vehicle Act, chapter 18, paragraph 187. It states: "It is a misdemeanor [heavy on the mean] to shoot at any kind of game bird or mammal, from an automobile or airplane." This does not seem unreasonable in California, where drive-by squirrel shootings were up almost 80 percent in the 1990s.

Illinois also found it necessary to create a statute that would nip squirrel harassment in the bud. General Statutes volume 2, page 1900, section 6138, is a law punishing, by fine or imprisonment, the throwing of snowballs at squirrels. Actually, the law specifically prohibits *boys* from throwing snowballs at trees and squirrels. I am sure it has been expanded and updated by now to include girls.

It is hard to say how these actions became laws, but the law does not insulate a squirrel from the actions of many vigilantes who feed birds. Squirrels are often thought of as nothing more than tree rats. As odd as it seems, there are many documented cases of people going off the deep end after being constantly challenged and bested by backyard squirrels.

A man in Kalamazoo, Michigan, was arrested for endangering himself and his neighbors, and unlawfully firing his rifle within city limits. The man went berserk, charging his bird feeder with his semiautomatic rifle blazing. He missed the squirrel, who leaped from the feeder and headed for the only safety he could find—the man's house, where the door had been left open (and we have already established that squirrels are opportunists). The man ran into the house in close pursuit, still firing as the squirrel traced a serpentine pattern from the kitchen to the living room, up and down the walls, and behind the furniture. When police arrived, the squirrel tore out of the house and right back to the bird feeder. After the man had been subdued, officers asked him why he had run through his house and fired fourteen rounds of ammunition at a squirrel. The reply: "Because I ran out of bullets."

Most cases are not this violent. A lot of people who feed birds, and object to feeding squirrels, simply walk softly and carry a big stick—usually a kitchen broom. Some are simply window knockers, while still others try verbal abuse.

A man in Missouri once told me that two elderly sisters who lived next door called him one day and asked if he could keep his squirrels at home. They didn't mind feeding their own squirrels, but they didn't want to have to feed his also. He didn't quite know what to say, so he just agreed. A few days later he saw the sisters pull into his driveway in their '50s-model Nash Rambler. They got out of the car and started unloading what looked like dead squirrels. They placed the animals on his picnic table, then went to the door. Very politely, one sister said, "We have brought your squirrels home, and we would hope that you will keep them home in the future."

They went on to explain that they had put Sominex in the bird feeder, put all the squirrels to sleep, and then picked out his and delivered them.

Additives in the bird feeder are not recommended. Although there are products on the market that are supposed to keep squirrels out of your feeder, these additives were not originally developed for squirrel prevention. Natural cayenne pepper additives, for example, were actually developed for the poultry industry, to keep rats out of chicken feed. Someone had the bright idea that it would also keep squirrels out of the birdseed. One problem with this product is that all the cayenne pepper settles to the bottom of the feeder, so one company began binding the powder directly to the seed. The UPS man showed up at my door one day with thirty pounds of this seed additive, sent by the manufacturer for me to try. I mixed it according to the instructions and watched as my whole day shift gave it the taste test. They all had the same reaction—after a few bites, they were on the ground snorting dirt! My ground squirrels, red squirrels, gray squirrels, and fox squirrels all took a few bites and went off like the *Challenger* spacecraft. But a few minutes later, they were back and loving it. I knew my night shift (an overweight mother raccoon and her babies) would be showing up on schedule. I didn't even mix the stuff; I just poured it into the feeder tray. Mama 'coon didn't even eat the seed; she just lapped up the cayenne powder. By coincidence, or by the manufacturer's design, I received a call from a reporter with the *Wall Street Journal* just a week later. He was doing a story on squirrels and at one point wanted to know what I thought of the cayenne pepper additive. I told him that within five minutes my squirrels were at the door asking for Dos Equis beer. After talking to me for forty-five minutes, that's the only quote he gave me.

The manufacturer was not too happy about my Dos Equis quip in the *Journal*. In fact, he called to explain to me that squirrels had to develop a dislike for his product. I said, "Now there is a marketing technique!"

The old joke about the woman who killed her husband with a hammer because he wouldn't eat his poison mushrooms doesn't work in the squirrel kingdom. Squirrels can eat mushrooms and other plants that are poisonous to humans without getting sick, apparently because they have a short digestive tract. Pepper additives to a squirrel are like condiments at Taco Bell. It's comparable to their having a bird feeder deluxe.

Can you harm a squirrel psychologically? One of the most often used tactics to discourage squirrels from partaking of seed purposely set out to attract songbirds is psychological warfare. It can be harmful to squirrels, but in most cases it turns out to be more harmful to those applying the treatment.

I heard from a woman in Ohio whose husband bought a remote-controlled model dune buggy at Radio Shack and operates it from the kitchen table. He keeps the dune buggy hidden in the bushes and watches for squirrels to start across the yard toward his bird feeder. When the squirrels get really close to the feeder, the man throws the remote-controlled vehicle in gear and has it peel out across the yard after them. A squirrel could almost have a coronary as he is pursued around the yard and over the neighbor's fence. The man then slowly backs the buggy into the bushes and fiendishly awaits more action.

It sounds like a good idea, but his wife is worried. Since her husband retired, she says, "This is all he does." She asked me if I thought she should hide the dune buggy. I told her, "No, he will know you did it. Hide the squirrels!"

I was teaching Bird Feeding 101 at a local college to a class full of seniors with squirrel problems. One gentleman explained to me that he thought for sure he had solved his squirrel dilemma by placing his feeder under the eave of his house. He had a wide eave that allowed him to set his feeder back almost three feet. He observed from the kitchen for several days as the squirrels leaned over from the eave trough, glaring at him and drooling over the feeder they could not conquer.

Soon, one of the squirrels began hanging upside down from the eaves trough by his rear claws, just staring at the feeder, which was still much too far away to reach. A week convinced the man that he had finally won. The very next morning his wife told him he had better do more research. As he watched in horror, the squirrel that had so often hung from the eaves trough started swinging his upside-down body back and forth until he had enough momentum to let go with his hind claws and angle himself through the air to the prize.

I have often wondered why the manufacturers of sound-bite bird feeders do not make them with two-way communications. These are bird feeders that have microphones built into them, allowing you to bring the sounds at the feeder into your home. If they were designed to deliver sound both ways, you could yell at your squirrel without ever leaving the comfort of your living room.

"He's going to hurt himself one of these days!"

When my daughter was born, we were given a Fisher-Price baby monitor as a gift. It worked wonderfully. We put it in her room, and when she fussed in the middle of the night, it immediately alerted us, and we could hear what was going on in her room. When we were done using the monitor, I taped the remote to the bird-feeder pole. It didn't save me any seed, but it was great entertainment to say BOO! to my squirrelly neighbors. When a squirrel first climbs onto a feeder and begins filling his face, he is very nervous. When he is nervous, he chews very rapidly. His eyes are located high and on each side of his head. This optic arrangement gives him a wide field of vision without his having to turn his head. I always waited until my squirrel began to relax. His chewing would slow dramatically and his eyes would shift less often. I would then quietly flip on the monitor and say, "GOOD MORNING, VIETNAM!" I just love that Robin Williams reaction from a squirrel.

Kids toys are possibly one of the best and cheapest forms

of squirrel-harassment equipment. If you can find one of
the jack-in-the-boxes with the timer at a secondhand store,
you have got one of the most inexpensive, up-to-date, high-
tech squirrel-harassment devices available on the market
today. When you put it out by the feeder, your squirrels are
going to be, at first, reasonably suspect. But time after time,
their love of food will override any new gadgetry gear fear.
If you have regulars at the feeder, timing should be no
problem at all. Just set the timer and position the box by
the feeder. It's better than BOO! When Jack jumps, your
squirrel jumps.

When company would come to the house, I used to set
the jack-in-the-box in a large box on the feeder pole and
sprinkle sunflower seed in the bottom of the box to attract
my squirrels. The squirrels would climb in to dine, but you
couldn't see them in the large
box. You also could not see
the jack-in-the-box when it
deployed. I told my guests
that I had a squirrel-in-a-
box and instructed them to
look at the box about the time
I knew Jack would jump.
When the jack-in-the-box
actuated, that squirrel would jump
straight into the air out of that box,
a good four feet.

I am not a sadistic person, but over
the years I have tried many methods
to keep squirrels out of my bird
feeders—not because
I thought any of them
would actually work, but
more to see why they
didn't. Some were more
entertaining than others.

**It's okay. It's just
another rabbit.**

Hanging a feeder up using heavy-test monofilament fishing line was a memorable experiment. I strung the line several feet out on an old horse chestnut tree limb. I placed it far enough out that I knew a squirrel could not jump from the tree trunk to the feeder that was hanging on the end of the line. I tied the feeder off about twenty feet down from the limb, just close enough to the ground so that I could reach it to fill.

Many squirrels gave a glance and passed on this seed outlet. But one young buck decided he would dine or die trying. The beauty of using monofilament fishing line is the fact that squirrels cannot grip it. This stud would wrap his paws around the line and ease himself all the way onto it. By the time he hit the feeder, he was doing Mach 4. He would collide with the feeder and crash to the ground. He would then sit there beneath the feeder and look around in dismay and disgust. Shortly, he would climb back to the top and try again—and again, and again, and again. Eventually he could hit the feeder at a full-throttle free fall and hang on for dear life. Even if it means an Excedrin headache, your squirrels will persist—and they will eat your seed.

Review and Relate

- Red squirrels will often live in abandoned woodpecker holes.
- Some squirrels will change coats twice a year.
- Fleas often become so thick and annoying in a squirrel nest that the mother is forced to move her family to another site. She does this by carrying the babies, one at a time, in her mouth. She grasps the babies at the belly with her mouth, allowing the youngster to wrap its feet around her head and neck for the ride to the new den.
- The biggest problem with squirrels is that they do not come with instructions.
- Squirrels are tone deaf and cannot hear sound made by pounding on window glass.

- The word *rodent* comes from the Latin *rodere,* "to gnaw."
- Ten percent of the squirrel population gets 90 percent of the seed, even though only 50 percent of the population requires help getting past baffled feeders.
- Squirrels are obligated to take a two-hour refresher course each year to help them distinguish between telephone wires and high-power electrical lines.
- Black squirrels tend to show up best on light-colored bird feeders.
- Researchers say squirrels claim a territory of one to several acres—urinating on trees to mark it, and trying to keep other squirrels from trespassing. Many of us have squirrels that evidently live in communes. If you have two dozen squirrels on your one-acre lot, your squirrels may be part of a cult.
- For the first few weeks after birth, squirrels are called naked. For the rest of their first year, they are called juvenile delinquents. After their first year, they become adults and are called Hairy Houdini.
- Squirrels are aggressive eaters with mild-mannered personalities.
- Squirrels do not always land on their feet like cats. They find it embarrassing to fall and usually will try to disguise any missteps.
- Squirrels can run eighteen miles per hour and chew at speeds up to one hundred, but they cannot run and chew at the same time.
- Squirrels will talk back. They have great communication skills, using high-pitched sound, tail quivering, and other body language. When a squirrel is flicking his tail, it is a sign that the squirrel is aggravated and the bird feeder is empty. Squirrels are products of their environments, so be careful what you say to your squirrel. He will soon be calling you whatever it is you have been calling him.
- It is hard to tell a male squirrel from a female. The only sure way is to look under the hood. I wouldn't suggest

turning your squirrel over. Entice him/her to run up a screen door, then take a quick look-see.

- There are four types of squirrel: the ground squirrel, the tree squirrel, the flying squirrel, and the bird-feeder squirrel.
- The squirrel has been traced back over 50 million years through fossil records. Early man used to chase squirrels with crudely made brooms.
- A true albino squirrel has pink eyes. Most white squirrels are not albino; the gene pool dictates the animals' color phase. Although most are mutations, some have been scared so badly by mean-spirited people that they actually turn white from worry and excessive related stress.
- Squirrels account for over 35 percent of all present-day mammals. Most of them live in your yard.
- If you think your squirrels could be causing an explosive situation in your backyard, remember, peanuts are one of the ingredients of dynamite.
- A squirrel's greatest enemies list includes humans, bob-cats, cats, dogs, coyotes, foxes, hawks, owls, snakes, rac-coons, weasels, brooms, and cars.
- Squirrels bury seeds, thereby planting trees for humans. Squirrels are also useful to humans as dinner, fur coats, and the butt of roadkill jokes.
- Squirrels use their tails for balance, as a parachute, as a shade for the sun, as a rudder, to signal danger to other squirrels, and as a wrap for warmth. They also use them quite unsuccessfully to flag down cars.
- Squirrels chatter among each other; namely, to sound the alarm if danger is nearby or someone with a broom is lurking around the corner of the house.
- A mother squirrel usually has two litters a year. Squirrel babies are furless at birth. It takes four to five weeks until their eyes open and they see what kind of mess they've gotten themselves into.

Tree Rat Trivia

THINGS YOU SHOULD KNOW ABOUT SQUIRRELS

1. Where do squirrels go when they die?
2. How does a squirrel mark his territory?
3. Why do squirrels dance in the middle of the road?
4. What is the cause of most squirrel bites?
5. Do squirrels fight?

THINGS YOU THOUGHT YOU KNEW ABOUT SQUIRRELS

1. What are young squirrels called?
2. Does the male squirrel help raise the young?
3. Why do squirrels hide their food?
4. What is the largest North American tree squirrel?
5. Are squirrels just tree rats?

THINGS YOU WISH YOU NEVER KNEW ABOUT SQUIRRELS

1. Where is the most populated squirrel area in North America?
2. What steps can you take to keep squirrels out of your bird feeder?
3. How fast will squirrels' teeth grow?
4. How can you tell if your squirrel has a drinking problem?
5. Why did the squirrel cross the road?

Trivia Answers

Things you should know about squirrels: 1. Stew? Squirrel heaven? I know where a lot of people would like them to go. In a natural setting they are usually eaten by predators. The few that are lucky enough to die from natural causes most likely expire at a bird feeder near a senior center. 2. Squirrels will defend their territory with force and harassment in some cases. They also mark trees on what they consider their turf by urinating. This works just fine unless a bigger urinator comes along and resets the boundaries. 3. A squirrel's erratic actions while crossing a road are a futile attempt to confuse an oncoming vehicle. These actions designed to convince the vehicle to change lanes just flat out don't work most of the time. 4. Hand-feeding almost always leads to a squirrel bite. Squirrels' eyes are always looking for predators, and they rarely focus on what they are eating. A squirrel can't tell where the jelly sandwich stops and your cute little fingers start. 5. When they are young they wrestle like all kids do. As adults they are not very aggressive. They will bite at each other when there is a confrontation over a food item. **Things you thought you knew about squirrels:** 1. They are called simply babies or infants when born. For the next six months they're referred to as juveniles. After that they become juvenile delinquents. 2. No, the male goes through two reproductive stages—lust and wanderlust. 3. For the same reason you do—to protect it from other family members. 4. Fox squirrel. 5. Squirrels and rats are both rodents, but they are not closely related— at least neither will admit it. **Things you wish you never knew about squirrels:** 1. The largest concentration of squirrels in North America is in Washington, D.C. (how did I know that already?); specifically, in Lafayette Park across from the White House. Some call it the "Squirrel Capital of the World." Squirrels roam free and are well fed by the thousands of well-fed feds on lunch break—that is, most of the time. Government employees have a lot of time and peanuts on their hands. 2. Long ones, brother, long ones. 3. Their incisors will grow almost six inches per year due to constant wear from bird feeders. 4. The hummingbird feeder is chewed in half. 5. To find out what those chickens were eating.

Big Hairy Deal

GRAY SQUIRREL

Some of you are very close to your squirrels, and I am sure you bring them in and measure them occasionally on the kitchen door to see how they have grown. This information will help you gauge where your squirrels should be in their development.

Day 1	Blind, pink, closed ears, beginning to dream about birdseed.
Day 2	Ear flaps unfolded, landing gear beginning to drop.
Week 1	Distinct whiskers, beginning to smell seed on parents' breath.
Week 2	Back dark, not pink; fur shows on head and muzzle.
Week 3	Fur; ear canals begin to open; two incisor teeth cut in lower jaw.
Week 4	Fur on top; underside still bare; upper teeth coming in; eyes begin to open.
Week 5	Learning to stand; beginning to nibble; needs milk.
Week 6	Grinding teeth out, eyes focusing on bird feeders.
Week 7	Peeks outside nest; still on milk.
Week 10	Gradually takes stolen solid food; goes out more.
Week 12	Can barely crack a nut, but is already spending time at the bird feeder.

"Say three Hail Marys and do not throw rocks
or use profanity on your squirrels again!"

CHAPTER FOUR

Getting the Best (and the Worst) of Your Squirrel

The squirrel-proof marketing ploy. A good salesman will tell you anything to make a sale. In the bird-feeding industry that *anything* is usually, "Oh yeah, this feeder is squirrel-proof." Most recently, I had a feeder manufacturer give me a pitch on a feeder with a timer. She said, "With this feeder you set the timer, and the feeder doles out a specific amount of seed at the time you designate. The purpose of this technology is so that you can be in the vicinity to watch when your feathered friends are partaking of the seed you offer." I said, "Let me see if I understand. This feeder trains squirrels to show up at the feeder at a given time each day." There was a slight pause. But being a smooth salesperson, she quickly recovered and started making up a great theory on how this feeder foils furballs.

The truth of the matter is, nothing is squirrel-proof. They will come in on stilts and hang gliders if they have to, but they *will* eat your seed! Squirrel-proof-bird-feeder salespersons are no different from the historically successful snake-oil salesperson. Snake oils would not always cure, but many times they made people feel better about their situation. Same goes for squirrel-proof devices. I'm not saying, Don't buy them. I'm saying, Don't expect miracles from them. Where there's a will, there's a way. And where there's a way, there's an annoying little rodent with an overbite that will find it or die trying.

Squirrels are forever linked to bird feeding. They became the nemesis of the backyard only after people started putting out seed for birds. All the devices we discuss in this book that have been designed to thwart them have come about through frustration. People are obsessive about trying to keep squirrels from eating their birdseed.

Persistence. It's hard to tell who are the most dedicated bird-feeder testers, the industry or the squirrels. The average gray squirrel can jump nine feet sideways, four feet straight up, and down twenty feet—then hang on where he lands. That gives you some idea about where to locate the bird feeders. The feeder should be more than nine feet from a tree or building; it should not be under anything from which a squirrel can easily jump. And if the feeder is on a pole, it should be protected by a squirrel baffle at least twenty inches wide and a squad of marines.

Feeders hanging in the open from a horizontal wire, protected by loose sleeves of small-diameter plastic pipe, can prevent a lot of pillaging. If the swiveling pipe sections are twenty inches long or more, most tightrope-walking squirrels cannot jump across, and watching the animals try to hang on is very entertaining.

The list of antisquirrel measures that don't work is not a sad commentary on human ingenuity—it is a glowing example of just how smart and efficient a squirrel is.

Baffle bluff. Let me start out by admitting that squirrel baffles, mounted on poles, will work under the best of conditions. The reason most of these contraptions fail is poor planning. If you place a baffled feeder within jumping range of a squirrel, it will simply launch to the feeder for lunch and never have to deal with the gauntlet of baffles you arranged. If you place your baffled feeder out away from the house, trees, fences, and other launching pads, it will force the squirrel to climb the pole and be buffaloed by the baffle. The problem is, once you move the feeder out far enough to foil your furball, you can't see the birds you were trying to attract in the first place. So when you buy that first baffle, make sure it comes with a free pair of binoculars.

Stovepipe is often used for baffle material. The problem with stovepipe is that once it begins to rust, it creates traction for squirrels that attempt to climb it. A better choice would be PVC pipe. It will not rust and becomes slicker when wet from rain or snow. You can mount either pipe material to the bottom of your feeder using S hooks. Greasing the pole or baffle material is not a good idea; grease and cooking oil sprays will actually harm squirrels, matting their fur in severly cold weather and causing them discomfort or possible death from hypothermia.

The baffle can become part of the feeder itself. On tube feeders, it is usually an umbrella device that domes the feeder. You can build your own Plexiglas baffle beneath your feeder very inexpensively. Take four pieces of Plexiglas and create a skirt around the bottom edge of your platform feeder. Once the squirrel climbs to the top of the pole, he then has to figure out how to deal with this clear plastic barrier that surrounds him.

Another recycling idea is to use an old metal garbage can lid or child's snow saucer as a baffle. A baffle this wide bought commercially can run as high as $100.

There are spring-loaded poles on the market that claim squirrel superiority. The pole is sleeved with a larger-diameter tube that is spring-activated. The weight of the squirrel when he jumps to the pole makes the sleeve drop and scares or throws the squirrel off the pole a couple times. But then the squirrel figures out why he is getting jilted and adjusts his jump.

Another baffle that is often overlooked is the 1950s toy the Slinky. A squirrel really has a hard time trying to understand what this is all about. Many young squirrels have never seen a Slinky and find it very frustrating to climb over. Some things just never give, but a Slinky never gives in. The more a squirrel tries to climb over it, the more it cascades down the pole.

Baffles that try to protect the feeder from air attack are sometimes effective. One on the market shaped like a witch's hat might keep the rain off your feeder, but it certainly won't keep your squirrels off. When a squirrel is puzzled, he immediately begins to chew on the problem until he figures it out. To begin chewing, all he needs is an edge. If you want a domed baffle that is not doomed before you get it out of the box, buy one without an edge. Look for a rounded top that does not give a squirrel the luxury of a foothold and the opportunity to begin chewing.

Some baffles are darkened. The theory here is that squirrels will not want what they cannot see. This is pretty shady marketing. If it were true, we could just outfit our squirrels with dark Blues Brothers glasses. The problem is, most squirrels can smell birdseed a mile away and will eat using the braille method if they have to.

If you have a hanging feeder that is adequately baffled, you are still not safe. A squirrel will often give up trying to land on and occupy a feeder. If the situation necessitates bouncing or head banging, it is not beneath a squirrel to resort to either. You can always tell when a squirrel is getting upset. He will start to twitch. His twitching will cause the line holding the feeder to move. The squirrel then wiggles the feeder a bit more, and some seed falls to the ground. The more a squirrel can dislodge, the harder he makes it sway. Soon, he gets impatient and dives directly at the feeder, giving it a body block that would knock down a Denver Bronco fullback. The bump and run never worked so well as for a squirrel. A squirrel is not after your feeder; he is after your seed. It doesn't matter how he gets it.

Nixalite is a material that looks much like a sea urchin. It has hundreds of sharp spines that project out like the pins on a pincushion. Attaching this to various feeder parts prevents squirrels from jumping to that location—but if you use enough of it, your beautifully designed bird feeder will look like a cactus.

One of the most efficient baffles would be a wide seed tray beneath the bird feeder. This kills two squirrels with one stone, so to speak. First, it catches seed the birds spill from the feeder. When it is not allowed to reach the ground, it won't attract tree squirrels and ground squirrels. Being wide, the tray acts as a baffle if the squirrel attempts to climb onto the pole. These seed trays are usually wide, circular, and flat. But unless it's located far enough away from objects that squirrels can launch from, a seed tray will become a landing platform equivalent to an aircraft carrier.

If you would like to baffle your bird feeder, but you don't want to spend a lot of money, go to the secondhand store and buy an umbrella. Open the umbrella and cut the shaft off as high as possible. String the umbrella on a wire before you hang your feeder. This will keep the seed dry, the birds happy, and your squirrels singing in the rain.

Some people swear by the fruit tin method of squirrel prevention. An inverted thirty-pound fruit tin works the same way every other baffle is supposed to work, except that it is free if you live in fruit country. The squirrel runs up the pole inside the fruit can and is stymied. One problem with this idea is that the world has now moved into the plastic age. Most fruit tins have been replaced with square plastic containers that stack better. Try to find a metal fruit tin. A squirrel can chew through a plastic fruit container before you get back to the house. If you can find a metal fruit container, it works better than stovepipe because it has a larger diameter.

Soda bottle baffles are also touted as squirrel-proof. The idea is to cut out the bottoms of a few empty two-liter plastic soda bottles and slide them up the bird-feeder pole or string the bottles along a wire that holds the bird feeder. This can work in certain situations, but many squirrels have learned that the best way around a well-engineered squirrel deflector is momentum and acceleration.

A squirrel is no different from a Ram Set. If you have ever worked construction, you have seen a tool that drives aluminum nails through steel I-beams. The way it works is acceleration. The nail is driven with the firing of a .22-caliber bullet. A squirrel is driven by desire, which gives it penetrating power almost unheard of in any other species. If a squirrel can go fast enough and quick enough past a baffle, momentum will eliminate any need for a good foothold or balance. Squirrels are on the top of the list of high achievers. (I don't know if they get that way using logic or logistics, but whatever it is, I wish I could can it.)

You can always "pot" your squirrel. I don't mean compost him; I mean baffle him with flowerpots. The way you do this is by connecting two flowerpots together at their bases and stringing them above your bird feeder. Keep in mind that any baffle object you use above a feeder must be much wider than the feeder itself. Otherwise, the squirrel will simply free-fall from the baffle and Velcro himself to the feeder on the way down.

Aluminum clothes-dryer pipe was originally designed to vent hot air safely out of homes. It is now used to vent squirrels. If you use four-inch pipe, squirrels have a hard time climbing it. This does not mean that they won't stand on each other's shoulders to reach the feeder. It works only on unimaginative squirrels.

Sound devices. We have discussed monitors that allow you to communicate with your squirrels from inside the house, but yelling can become boring quickly. Using a baby monitor, two-way radio, or other inexpensive communications device, try adding creative sounds. You will get more than your money's worth of entertainment from a sound effects tape that you play for your squirrels. When your squirrels jump to the feeder perch and hear a train coming through or automatic machine-gun fire, I guarantee laughter. Squirrels hit the ground running at full throttle all the way across the yard, then stop and look back in disbelief.

Most squirrels realize right away that this can't be for real. No sooner do they get used to trains and machine guns, when all of a sudden a 747 comes through and a ferryboat foghorn starts blasting away. The best reaction comes with the screaming hawk sounds. Most squirrels think they have bought the farm. Many times they don't even run; they stay right at the feeder, kneel, and pray.

You don't have to feel guilty about scamming your squirrels. They are con artists of the highest mammalian order. A squirrel can con a corn kernel from a canary, and does it every chance he gets. Squirrels will frustrate you constantly. If you can best them just once in a while, you will get a warm feeling all over. Squirrels love to be challenged. If you do not occasionally test their limitations, they become bored and depressed. I am very tolerant of my squirrels and all their antics, but one thing that really annoys me is nectar snatching. They have a bad habit of slipping down to my hummingbird feeders and slurping the sugar water. I wouldn't mind their bootlegging a little beverage, but they chew holes in my hummer feeders to siphon the nectar faster. Squirrels are hyper enough without giving them a sugar rush. I nipped the problem in the bud by first filling my hummingbird feeders with prune juice, which quickened their step a bit, and then offering them their own easy-access nectar feeder with large openings. This squirrel nectar feeder turned out to be a magnet that attracted some fifty species of birds that also needed the larger openings to sip sugar water.

Noisemakers. If you have any false hopes that noise or noise devices will control squirrels that annoy you, don't spend big money to find out that this is a myth. Yelling and window knocking can demonstrate what little effect noise has on squirrels. The high-pitched silent noisemakers sold in catalogs and late-night television ads are a joke. If they really worked, wouldn't they drive your dog nuts? The only noise these gadgets make is when the seller puts your coins in his pocket. If the human ear can't hear these high-pitched noises, who's to say they make any noise? Whether they do or not is beside the point. The question is, Will it thwart squirrels? If you can't see the bird feeder through all your visiting squirrelly neighbors, I am guessing it doesn't. If it did bother squirrels, they would probably show up wearing earmuffs, or you would be hearing them talking louder to each other. The only squirrel frequency I am aware of is "regularly at the feeder."

Another sound device is the cannon, and I don't mean army-issue, I mean the ones used at airports to scare birds off the runway. Most are air-compression cannons that fire at regular intervals. I would imagine that they work fine out in the middle of an airport taxiway, but I'm betting you would have some complaint problems with your neighbors if you had one going off every five minutes in your back-yard! Is shell shock worth it to save a few sunflower seeds? Most battle-weary squirrels wouldn't be bothered by it anyway—although I'm sure all the birds you are trying to attract would quickly fly away.

Trying to brainwash your squirrels with subliminal messages will not work either. It is impossible to override a squirrel's evolutionary response to food.

Wiry squirrels. Matching wits with a squirrel can be very humbling. Perhaps one of the oldest tricks used to thwart squirrels is a wire stretched between two objects with a seed outlet placed somewhere near the middle. If you know little about squirrel ability, you would probably string a wire and think you were safe. The reality of the situation is that stringing the wire is only the first line of defense. A squirrel can wire-walk right side up or hand-over-foot upside down. A wire or rope alone will not deter a squirrel for more than a millisecond. Even thin piano wire will not stop most squirrels.

The next obvious step is to place baffles along the wire

that challenge a squirrel charge. Wire baffles could include plastic pipe, plastic milk jugs, pie tins, beads, soda cans, old records, coffee cans, plant supports—anything round that will throw your squirrels off balance. Historically, the problem with this method is that squirrels are very well balanced. They look at this situation as a log-rolling contest. Some very intelligent squirrels will use the physics of acceleration to gallop across the wire and its many devices without so much as turning an ankle. If your engineering skills are poor, a squirrel will jump over the objects you put before him. Never use nylon rope in place of wire. Frustrated squirrels will eventually wise up and chew the rope at one end, sending all your greatest ideas—and your birdseed—to the ground.

If you use a wire-suspended method of bird-feeder hanging, wire tension is very important. There is no such thing as being too tense when you are dealing with squirrels. If the wire is too loose, the objects you string along the wire all collide and become less effective.

One interesting idea is to cut both ends out of coffee cans and string eight of them along a wire, four on each side of the feeder. The squirrels will soon attempt to crawl upside down along the wire or walk on top of the wire. When they get to the cans, they either go over, under, around, or through. Whichever way they choose becomes so difficult, it makes their heads spin—

"A little more to the right, Lefty!"

along with the rest of their bodies. This proves that people drink too much coffee. It keeps them up all night, trying to brainstorm ways to keep squirrels down all day.

Beer garden. Putting a container of beer in the garden will attract slugs that are after your plants. Once the slugs crawl into the beer, they drown before they have a chance to share in your bounty. Many gardeners who have tried this slugfest method find their squirrels having a tough time negotiating the tree limbs. Squirrels end up taking slugs from the garden, but not the kind the gardener had in mind. Anything you put outside can and will be used against you in a courtyard of squirrels. Everything becomes squirrel food unless you take steps to stop them, and sometimes steps are the only thing that will work.

A recent experiment using the psychological response theory (PRT) has proven hopeful. Some feel it could be a breakthrough in squirrel rehabilitation. By using an ordinary lightbulb, scientists were able to program the test squirrels to feed only when the light was on. They did this by augering a small amount of sunflower seed into feeders

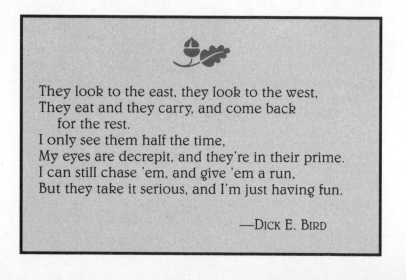

They look to the east, they look to the west,
They eat and they carry, and come back
    for the rest.
I only see them half the time,
My eyes are decrepit, and they're in their prime.
I can still chase 'em, and give 'em a run,
But they take it serious, and I'm just having fun.

—DICK E. BIRD

and then turning the light on each time. Squirrels were soon coming to the feeder only when the light was on. It took squirrels very little time to figure out that no light meant no seed. To make this work for you would mean an intensive retraining program for your squirrels, but your seed savings could be significant. Once your squirrels have been trained in PRT, you just turn the light off and leave it off. It will mean years of field study before it is known how long this method will keep squirrels in the dark. Lab squirrels tend to be more lenient and patient.

Projectiles. Throwing and shooting things at your squirrels can be very labor-intensive, but some people have nothing better to do. I have heard of people throwing Frisbees, snowballs, and water balloons at squirrels. A woman in Minnesota divorced her husband because she said all he ever did was shoot marshmallows at squirrels on the bird feeder with his slingshot. High-powered, battery-operated water guns that fire a stream of water over fifty feet have often been used to harass but never deter a squirrel hooked on birdseed.

A woman in Connecticut built a hawk silhouette out of plywood and hung it from a Tarzan rope in her backyard. She would pull the hawk up into a nearby tree and tie it off with a slipknot. When her feeder became lopsided from too many furballs, she would loosen the hawk and it would swoop down over the feeder. Squirrels ran into each other trying to flee. This worked great until one day when she didn't notice her husband—home early from work—crossing the yard. The plywood hawk caught him in the back of the head. At the same time, he tripped over several panic-stricken squirrels and landed on top of the nearby birdbath, which collapsed beneath him. The medical bill for a broken ankle and slight concussion would have fed their squirrels nicely for several years.

"Yes, 911? I would like to report a drive-by shooting."

Some people never grow up. Some people revert to their childhoods after retirement. A man in Ohio, having become very upset with squirrels raiding and destroying his new bird feeder, tried to solve his problem with a toy weapon he remembered from his childhood. He and his childhood chums built rubber-band rifles out of wood and crafted ammunition from old inner tubes, which made giant rubber bands when cut crosswise. They then stretched them across their wooden rifles and attached them to spring-loaded clothespins. The bands shot several yards and were harmless. He decided to use this weaponry on his squirrels, which put him in the hospital. It worked pretty well on his squirrels, though; they actually ran from the feeder as soon as they saw him with the rubber-band gun. In fact, it worked so well he became bored. One day he noticed his wife bent over in the garden near the bird feeder and couldn't resist the tempting target. He made a bull's-eye but got more than he bargained for. The first rule of engagement being fire superiority, his wife quickly recovered from her shock, grabbed the water hose, and returned fire. In his haste to retreat, her husband fell over backward in his lawn chair and sprained his back. His wife told the paramedics that it was an old injury from the great squirrel war.

Fenced-in food. Manufacturers and do-it-yourself home craftsmen have decided that the best defense is a good offense. To accomplish this they have designed barricaded bird feeders, using heavy wire mesh. There are several designs, but all feature a bird feeder encased in small-diameter-opening wire mesh. The idea is that a bird can squeeze in and out, but a squirrel just hangs on the bars, trying to extend his reach until he dislocates a shoulder. A squirrel is not known to use tools in an effort to gain access to seed, but leverage is definitely part of a squirrel's understanding of physics. Dumping seed is the normal method a squirrel will use to foil a feeder of this type. If the feeder is attached to a cord or loosely mounted, a squirrel will make short work of turning it upside down or knocking it off the mount to spill the beans.

Utility poles. Long before a manufacturer actually began marketing a bird feeder that was designed to deliver a trickle shock to squirrels, homeowners used battery chargers hooked to their bird-feeder poles. This does baffle a squirrel, both mentally and physically for a while, but squirrels tend to take the path of least resistance. Squirrels get a real charge out of vaulting voltage. They are persistent in their attempts to mount the feeder. Each time one gets nipped by your energized feeder, he learns *what not to touch* in his next attempt. An electrified feeder pole is no more squirrel-proof than a baffled pole if a squirrel can jump around or over it.

The problem with the very expensive commercial feeders

that promise to shock your squirrel into submissiveness is—power outages. The feeders are battery operated, and the power demand zaps the small battery in a matter of hours. The manufacturer will tell you that the feeder is designed to act much as a shock training collar works on a hunting dog. The squirrel is supposed to learn that stealing seed means a volt jolt. The problem is, the battery always runs out before the squirrel graduates from this school of thought.

The inverted fishbowl feeder. When you buy a feeder that you are convinced is squirrel-proof, there are other factors to consider. The most important consideration should be the needs of the birds you are trying to attract to the feed that you are trying to keep from your furballs. Many feeders that attempt to deny access to squirrels also deny access to larger, desirable birds.

Clear plastic feeders designed so that small songbirds must flutter up into them are a case in point. They do a great job of keeping squirrels out of the birdseed but also restrict usage to all but the small songbirds that can flutter up into the seed-outlet areas. Feeders designed with adjustable baffles create the same problem. The lower the baffle is set, the fewer birds that can access it. Squirrels use a trial-and-error method of requisitioning what they want. As long as they know there is food available, they will never stop trying to reach it. Any feeder that seems to be working at thwarting your squirrels should be securely fastened to something. One of the last alternative methods a squirrel will use, after everything else has failed, is to knock the feeder off center to spill seed or knock it to the ground completely and deal with it on an equal footing.

Smells. Putting naphthalene (mothballs) in the garden to drive off rabbits or around the feeder to dispel squirrels is basically a waste of good mothballs. If this really worked, wouldn't they be called hareballs or furballs? Mothballs are to dispel moths! A lot of squirrel-proof ideas stink. This one, not unlike the use of fox urine, sounds good—even makes sense; the problem is, it doesn't work in the field.

Combination foilers. If you need convincing that squirrel-proof feeders do not really work, look at models that offer more than one squirrel barrier. Some companies are marketing bird feeders with baffle skirts, wire-mesh enclosures, and perch-activated trays. This has to tell you that each of these ideas alone failed miserably. One model has all the above plus a solar-powered electronic brain that generates a mild pulse. Birds can't feel the pulse, but squirrels (and humans) find it uncomfortable. I watched one day as one of my squirrels sunned himself on the solar wafer (blocking the energy that charges the feeder), while the other skipped rapidly through the gauntlet of baffles and filled his face.

Platform feeders. Flat, shelflike feeders have always been easy targets for squirrels. They are designed to feed a lot of birds in an open environment. Usually, a roof is attached to keep rain and snow from soaking the seeds. One patented idea was to layer the platform with close-tolerance screening, which would allow birds to reach in with their beaks but not allow for a squirrel's paw. If the squirrel cannot simply tip the platform over and spill the seed out, it would almost seem foolproof—unless you know squirrels.

Most manufacturers never figure into their engineering equations the "animal inner-action factor." If there truly were a design that did not allow access to a squirrel, do you really think those little fuzz faces would throw their paws in the air and surrender? No way! As in the case of this feeder, squirrels simply go to plan B.

Plan B usually has something to do with intimidation. The squirrel sits on or near the feeder and waits for a bird to extract a seed. The squirrel bluff-charges, and the bird drops his dinner on departure. This is called the "bait-and-switch bird bluff." It works every time. Birds never get tired of prying seed out of feeders, and squirrels never get tired of prying seed out of birds.

Squirrel toys. In the past several years, more and more squirrel toys have come on the market. Unheard of at one time, these entertaining devices have now become popular with those who have almost given up trying to keep fuzzy-faced little rodents out of the birdseed.

Estate planning for your squirrels is not so far-fetched. You should think of your squirrels' future. You aren't going to be around forever. The best thing you can do for your squirrels is challenge them, and squirrel toys are just another way to exercise your squirrels while you feed them. The most famous design is the squirrel whirler, shaped like a Ferris wheel with a corncob at the end of each strut. As the squirrel climbs to the targeted cob, the wheel gives in to gravity and rolls down. The squirrel swings down with the cob but usually falls off the first couple of tries. All that corn is just too tempting to leave. It takes a squirrel about three minutes to master this wheel of fortune. Before long, the squirrel is able to ride the cob to the bottom and still hang on and eat it. Soon the squirrel learns to climb aboard the cob that is already on the bottom of the wheel. The entertainment comes into play when more than one squirrel tries dining on the wheel at once. This throws everyone's equilibrium off, and all kinds of food fights erupt.

There is also the squirrel feeder that I call the "stingy box." This is a simple wooden container with a hinged lid. Inside, you can put peanuts, birdseed, peanut butter, or suet. When the squirrels finally figure out it's a food box, they quickly learn to open the lid and help themselves. They love this feeder because most birds cannot get at the food. Once crows discover the box, however, the squirrels end up waiting in line. The box will also help you identify your dominant squirrel. She is the one that reaches in for food and then eats it while sitting on the lid. She will bluff-charge any other squirrel that tries to dine with her.

Squirrel toys are actually baffles purchased by those who do not want to admit defeat. It is a way of saving face. Instead of telling people, "My squirrel is smarter than I am," they say, "I love to feed the squirrels in my yard." These are people who have been outsmarted and are ashamed to admit it. Squirrel-toy owners are people in self-denial who have caved in to squirrel pressure.

Whether you call them baffles or toys, you will soon learn that squirrels study one item at a time. They rate obstacles in degrees of difficulty and assign solutions to memory. A squirrel never forgets a tactic once it is developed.

The squirrel trapeze is a corncob-holding toy that demonstrates a squirrel's skill in endurance and balance. The squirrel has to jump to the trapeze bar, which is made up of corncobs, and balance on it while eating. The squirrel jumps to the bar and hugs it with all four paws. The bar is designed as an axle so that the corn and the squirrel immediately turn upside down. The squirrel hangs on for dear life and starts chewing the bar. This is equivalent to climbing out on a tree branch and sawing it off behind you.

Squirrel toys like the teeter-totter, the slide, the monkey bars, the whirligigs, and the trapeze are all real cute, but they will not keep squirrels off your expensive feeders full of premium seed. Researchers have run several tests proving beyond a doubt that squirrels with an IQ of 120 or greater will not even play on these toys, and even the stupid ones stop for lunch.

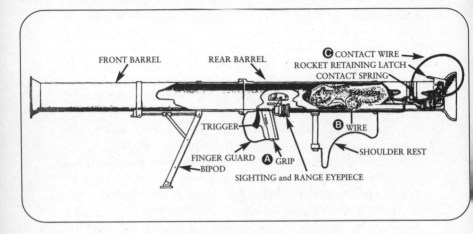

PARTS OF A BAZOOKA
SQUIRREL RELOCATOR

This cutaway of a bazooka squirrel relocator is loaded and ready for firing. When trigger on "A" grip is squeezed, an electric current is sent through the "B" wire to "C" contact wire. This ignites the propellant powder just behind the squirrel and launches him downrange.

Your best defense against squirrels still turns out to be feeding them and managing your feeding program. Successful management is giving them what they don't like and making them think they like it. You can make them think they like it by simply making them think you don't want to give it to them. Once they have it and think you don't like them to have it, you've made them take something you don't want. That's management!

Facing your squirrels. Trying to keep an eye on your squirrels without their realizing it has affected many people that feed birds. The eyes are the first to go, and some experts agree that it is from the constant strain on the directional eye muscles, which causes them to fatigue and involuntarily relax in a left or right position. Most agree that if the patient faced her squirrel and stared directly at him, this condition would never have afflicted her. You can tell when a person first begins to show signs of this ailment. When she is paying for her seed at the cash register, she begins to stand sideways more and more, talking out of the side of her mouth. (Don't embarrass anyone by asking; it could be that the poor soul is just drunk.) Studies are beginning to show that this is not just a physical problem: it's also psychological. Even with optic exercise, the treatment to correct this situation is not always totally successful. Many people just cannot bring themselves to face their squirrels, and the side-eye condition becomes dominant again as soon as they get back home.

Government intervention. It is illegal to kill a squirrel out of season—unless you work for the government. The government has its own set of rules. Government officials cannot possibly work under the strict enforcement they bind the rest of us in. If not for a dedicated group of animal rights activists in San Francisco, squirrels could be endangered there. The Contra Costa County chapter of In Defense of Animals once won a court order against the U.S. Navy, forcing the navy to suspend its squirrel-killing program. The squirrels were finding their way into the navy's ammunition bunkers. (Nothing is more dangerous than a heavily armed squirrel!) The navy scattered five tons of oats containing the anticoagulant chlorophacinone over an 800-acre site.

Not only did it kill many innocent squirrels, but it also killed everything else that would be attracted to the oats.

Crime scene tape. There comes a time when you have to say to yourself, Is this worth it? If your squirrels are determined to take over your yard, it might be wise to just cordon off your property line with yellow police tape and just give up. This has happened more than once in city parks around the country. A bumper crop of acorns can sometimes make squirrels hyperactive. This often produces a bumper crop of squirrels. Before long, up goes the yellow tape with accompanying signs that read, "Park closed due to overaggressive squirrels." In Wheaton, Maryland, Montgomery County's Regional Park was forced to close temporarily once. Two children were bitten, and one man said he had to bludgeon an attacking squirrel to death with a stick, in what he claimed was self-defense. (It is no wonder his wife sent him to the park.) A park without squirrels would be like a crime scene without yellow tape. It just wouldn't be natural.

Yard rage. When squirrels eat your flowers, chew your feeders, and break into your garage to help themselves to the birdseed bag, don't take it personally. They're just being squirrels, and when you think about it, battling with squirrels is useless. Unless you find some entertainment value in it, squirrel wars can be a self-destructive exercise. Just be glad they are outside.

Santa is not the only one using chimneys to gain entrance to homes. A woman in Toledo had a squirrel sneak into her home through the chimney stack and start a chain of events that almost wore her out. She spotted the furball in her living room and called the cops. When the cops showed up, the squirrel didn't. Animal control did a sweep of the house and found no sign of a squirrel. As the officer was about to leave, the woman spotted the squirrel behind her commode. The control officer used a toilet plunger handle to prod the squirrel. The squirrel panicked, the woman panicked, and then the officer panicked. Weapons were drawn. The officer fired his crowd-control pepper spray all over the bathroom as the squirrel ran serpentine across the walls, cabinets, and sink. The officer was temporarily blinded by his own pepper spray, the woman thought she was going to pass out, and the squirrel decided he didn't have to go to the bathroom after all.

Unable to catch the animal, the control officer left the woman a live trap and baited it with peanut butter. She sat up all night in bed with the light on watching the trap, but the squirrel never took the bait.

Fresh troops were sent in the following day. Three animal control people chased the squirrel around the woman's house for an hour before finally deciding to give up and again leave the live trap. Still holding a broom above her head, the woman said, "Hey, wait a minute. You can't leave me here alone with that critter." Not sure what the woman might do with the broom, the crew decided they would try one more time.

**"Come on, I saw a great big fat guy in a red suit
do it last month!"**

One officer thought he had the squirrel trapped under the freezer. He used a coat hanger to try snaring the culprit. As the officer lay flat on the floor, eyeball to eyeball with the squirrel, he tried to loop his wire around the little animal. The squirrel darted out from under the appliance, across the officer's face, and straight into the live trap full of peanut butter.

The woman could finally relax. But every time she hears a strange noise, she hopes it's only Santa.

The best method of removing a squirrel from a home is the use of a live trap. Once you have had squirrels in the house, you won't mind having them outside half as much. In some cases, they don't have to actually enter your home to cause damage.

In the Chicago suburb of Hinsdale, Illinois, a family contracted painters to scrape and repaint their new home. They had just finished the interior work and were out on the back deck cleaning under the eaves, putting primer on the exterior siding. One of the painters discovered a large ball of leaves beneath the eave and began to knock it down. The ball burst open with his first blow, and five squirrels jumped out at him. The painter was so shocked, he fell backward and overturned a five-gallon bucket of primer onto the deck. Panicked baby squirrels ran everywhere, the painters yelled, and a dog that had been napping under the deck yelped and howled. The owner opened the porch door to find out what was happening, and the panicked family dog ran into the house covered in primer. The woman yelled at the dog, which only made the poor mutt more confused as he ran upstairs, shaking paint off himself and rolling on the carpeting.

The typical evidence of tree squirrels in your home—besides noise—includes droppings, gnawed holes, nest materials, food stores, shells, hulls, pits, and other food remnants.

Decommoding. When most people think of baffling a squirrel, they are thinking about their bird feeders. In some cases, they should be thinking about their toilets. I hate to make you bladder-shy, but squirrels in toilets are not un-common. An adventuresome furball goes down the sewer vent, does a little jockeying Cousteau-style, and works his way right into the commode. One family I know was get-ting ready to go out, and both bathrooms were up to full capacity since everyone was showering and dressing. The squirrel ended up in the bathroom the two young daughters were using. When the squirrel made his cave-diving en-trance, bloodcurdling screams came from the bathroom as the girls made quick exits. Dad, thinking the house must be on fire, came busting out of his shower and raced for that end of the house. When he arrived on the scene, he was as wet as the squirrel, but the squirrel had more on than he did. Wrestlemania broke out, and the squirrel was finally wrapped in a towel and deposited outside.

Once an Arizona man heard splashing coming from the bathroom, and he was the only one home. Cautiously, he crept in and lifted the lid on the stool. A squirrel came out as if the stool had been a jack-in-the-box. Frozen in fear, the man watched this wet rodent make several 360-degree tours of the bathroom. Finally, the squirrel ended up in the tub, which he couldn't get back out of because of its slip-pery sides. Locking the squirrel in the bathroom, the man dashed to the garage and grabbed a large trash can. (Thinking fast on your feet does not always translate into great ideas.) Trying to scoop the squirrel out of the bathtub with the garbage can just didn't work. The squirrel saw this as an opportunity. He jumped on top of the garbage can and launched himself out into the master bedroom.

Admitting he was up against a greater mind than his own, the man decided to bring in reinforcements. He slammed shut the bedroom doors and called animal con-trol. He was expecting a SWAT team to show up to nego-tiate with the squirrel but instead was given advice. A very calm woman on the other end of the phone said the squirrel would take any chance offered to escape. She suggested opening a window and building a ramp so the squirrel could easily make his way out.

The guy said, "Great. I'm late for work and now I have to build a viaduct for a squirrel."

He couldn't just leave the window open and hope for the best. What if his wife came home and the squirrel was still in the bedroom? Instead, he chased the squirrel around the room with a broom for two hours, calling him terrible things. The squirrel did not want to leave. He had never had his own master bedroom before.

The guy finally angled the squirrel off the wall and out the window, as if he was playing a game of pool.

Finding a squirrel in your commode can leave deep psychological scars. There can be trepidation about returning to the scene of the crime. This man said he survived relatively unscathed. When he is at home and the need arises, he has no problem using the toilet—at the Amoco station two blocks away.

The lesson to be learned: screen the squirrels that use your bathroom by screening your plumbing vents. And next time you see your squirrel out on the bird feeder, don't get upset. Just be thankful he is away from the house. Squirrel traffic across wooden house siding en route to a bird feeder begins to show very quickly. Squirrels have sharp claws, and it doesn't take long for wear to show up on soft cedar siding. Locate feeders that attract squirrels away from the house.

Trapping and moving squirrels is not always the answer. Others will move into the territory, and you will have to start all over to build that grudge. You can deter some of the squirrels some of the time, and all of the squirrels some of the time, but you can never deter all of the squirrels all of the time.

Squirrelly mechanics. If your car is acting a little squirrelly, you might want to have your dealer check out the suspension. A couple in Ohio say their neighbor cut down an old rotting maple tree, and one of the hollow rotting branches came down facing their house. Out from this hollow marched a whole squirrel family. Since the first thing they saw was the couple next door, the squirrels assumed that these were the people who cut their tree down.

Soon after, the couple's car developed a terrible sound in its rear end. They had several costly checkups of things like the exhaust and shocks, which added to their expense with no solution. Finally they drove the car to a local Ford dealer, who after close inspection presented the couple with a huge walnut that had been lodged between the car's frame and its body.

So next time you think you are outsmarting your squirrel, remember—they never, ever forget.

Another bad habit squirrels have is loading up your car's catalytic converter with nuts. This gets very expensive. The little guys go spelunking through your exhaust system and come to this big room that looks like a perfect nut warehouse. Before long, your car is not running well, and mechanics cannot figure out why. Squirrels can be very exhausting.

Kleptomania. Has it ever occurred to you that your squirrel does not know he is stealing your bird feed, seed, suet, and nectar? Research has now shown that as many as 90 percent of North American squirrels suffer from kleptomaniac tendencies. The condition creates an irresistible impulse in squirrels to steal bird feed. It seems to occur more in city squirrels than rural individuals. Most researchers feel that the high percentage of kleptomania stems from emotional disturbances caused by people yelling at them, throwing things, and knocking on windows while they are trying to eat.

A squirrel who is not affected will simply sit quietly on the feeder and eat in a very normal manner. He chews his food in a relaxed position and takes small portions at a time. Those individuals suffering from kleptomania are very easy to spot. They eat in a rush, talk with their mouths full, fill their cheeks with all the seed they can possibly stuff in, and shift each eye separately, while simultaneously searching the yard for yellers, throwers, and knockers.

There is no known cure for kleptomaniac squirrels. Once a squirrel has been affected, his social behavior can never be reversed with any methods yet tried. Behavioral science has come a long way in the past several decades, and squirrel abnormalities are just beginning to get some recognition.

You can help in the effort to stamp out SK (squirrel kleptomania) worldwide. To begin with, we know that at least 10 percent of the squirrel population is not troubled by this emotional scourge. Let's stop it from spreading any further. Since it is so hard for a layperson to distinguish between a klepto and nonklepto, I suggest that you just quit yelling, throwing, and knocking altogether. By beginning a squirrel-feeding program in your yard, you will be helping to wipe out this condition once and for all. Backyards will once again be harmonious. This is what the world is working toward: peace, opportunity, and free meals. The world will be a better place when all the squirrels and all the nuts get together.

You will know the program is working successfully when your squirrel shows up at the feeder one day with no bag over his head, but two under his arms. He will take all he wants, but eat all he takes.

Control freaks. One thing you can do to slow up your furballs is to slow up your advertising. If you keep your seed corralled, it will not serve as a neon sign that says, Come and get it! I am not trying to convince you that squirrels will not find your feeder if there is no seed on the ground, but it will discourage those squirrels that are trying to quit by not tempting them. The catch-22 is that some seed catch trays act as squirrel perches, nice wide areas that a squirrel can really stretch out on and chow down.

Another thing that you can do is not look. What you can't see can't hurt you. When you go out and see the feeder empty, why assume a squirrel ripped you off? Assume the birds ended up with the seed. This is much less stressful and more gratifying.

Here you will find fifty of the great and not-so-great ideas and theories about baffling squirrels. They come from all over North America, the bright ideas of frustrated squirrel repellers who have not yet come to the realization that squirrels cannot be conquered. There is a higher intelligence, and it resides in squirrels!

1. Staple natural thornbushes to a wooden feeder pole. If you have a squirrel that is a thorn in your side, fight briar with briar. It doesn't hurt to needle your squirrel a bit.
2. String thread spools along a wire on each side of where the feeder is hanging. Metal plates need to be placed at

two-foot intervals because squirrels will cross the wire upside down, hand over hand, across the spools.

3. Guard dogs work very well to control squirrels. The most effective breed is the Australian shepherd. These dogs will herd your squirrels anywhere you choose.

4. You can keep your squirrels busy and out of trouble by attaching unshelled peanuts to the end of several strings and letting them hang from the end of a branch. Squirrels will quickly learn to slowly reel in the tethered goobers.

5. Velcro your squirrels and your feeder pole. The squirrels stick to the pole, and once a day you go out after dark and peel them off. The squirrels go straight home because they are afraid of the dark.

6. Install a sprinkler system in your yard with a motion sensor at the feeder pole. Direct a high volume of water at the pole. You will have a flood of complaints from your squirrels, but you will save enormous amounts of seed.

7. Squirrel-proof feeders take imagination. Don't confuse an imagination with an inventive mind. Nothing is actually squirrel-proof, so you need to spend a lot of time pretending there is. Thinking you are smarter than a squirrel feels just as good as being smarter than a squirrel.

8. One great way to rid yourself of squirrels, which works for some folks who do not deal well with reality, is to simply snap your fingers and they are gone. It is not just the snap that is effective—sometimes you have to say "Hey!" at the same time. You might also want to try "Bibbity, bobbity, boo!"

9. Blowguns—they're cheap, simple, and legal. Just a little practice with the dumdums on the dumb-dumbs, and you can hit a moving squirrel at thirty yards every time. You get the most surprised looks from not only your squirrels but also your neighbor's cat.

10. Greasing a feeder pole will kill your squirrel in cold weather. The grease mats the squirrel's insulating fur, and he dies of hypothermia. In some cases, however, grease increases traction. Greased poles become tacky in cold weather, and a squirrel just scampers up.

11. The University of Southwestern Rhode Island did a study showing that squirrels relocated less than two miles from home will return before the relocator.

12. Squirrel baffles work very well if your squirrels are mental midgets.

13. Squirrels have an uncanny ability to run at top speed along fence lines, telephone lines, clotheslines, power lines, and property lines. Obstacles along these corridors will slow their progress.

14. There is only one species of flying squirrel in your backyard, but the rest of them think they are. Locate feeders a good distance downrange from squirrel jumping-off points.

15. Squirrel teeth grow continuously from the roots and wear away at the tips. Only the front surfaces are protected by enamel, so the teeth wear faster on the backside. This back wear helps develop a sharp, chisel-like edge on the front of the teeth. Do not expect security from wood or plastic feeders. Use stainless steel.

16. Replace the plastic great horned owl on the feeder with a real one.

17. Squirrels, like birds, are very territorial. Placing a small mirror inside the feeder makes a squirrel go ballistic. He sees his reflection and thinks it is some other good-looking furball. The angrier he gets, the angrier the other guy gets, until finally they scare themselves away.

18. An optimist is one who thinks that birdseed prices cannot go any higher and that squirrels will quit eating the stuff. Be an optimist with a pessimist's pocketbook.

19. Marvel at the generosity of your squirrels, who so graciously allow your songbirds to dine with them in the harmony of nature.

20. Squirrels can be prevented from traveling on wires by installing a two-foot section of lightweight, two- to three-inch diameter plastic pipe. Slit the plastic pipe lengthwise and place it over the wire. The pipe will rotate with the weight of the squirrel, causing it to tumble. Do not use this method on electrical wires unless supervised by a qualified squirrel or someone from the power company.

21. Livetrapping could be necessary in some situations. Metal live traps are available from some farm and garden supply stores and numerous catalogs. Live-trapped squirrels should be released at least two or three (hundred) miles away to prevent their return.

22. To keep squirrels from eating your flowers, some suggest a solution of one teaspoon of Lysol or three ounces of Epsom salts added to one gallon of water. These sprays must be repeated frequently since new growth and rains reduce their effectiveness.

23. To make a squirrel baffle, start with a No. 3 coffee can that has one end removed. With tin shears, cut a hole the circumference of the bird-feeder pole into the center of the other end of the can. Next, put two screws into opposite sides of the pole, about eight inches below where the bottom of the feeder will be. Turn the coffee can upside down, then slide the can down over the top of the pole. The screws will hold the can in place. Put your feeder on top of the pole, then sit back and watch your feathered friends feast at your feeder—without interference from pesky squirrels. (This is guaranteed to work only on stupid squirrels.)

24. It is not true that a squirrel finds it impossible to navigate along link chain. In fact, squirrels find link chain a very convenient route to bird feeders. The chain offers easy gripping, and squirrels hang beneath and climb paw over paw until they can reach the seed. You can frustrate members of the chain gang by placing lightweight garden pots along the chain. The chain is fed through the center holes in the bottoms of the pots and allowed to spin freely. But it is blocked by a wire clip stopping the pots from coming within two feet of the food source. The open ends of the pots are assembled facing away from the feeder. The reason for keeping the pots two feet from the feed is that squirrels, suspended by their hind paws, can swing like monkeys to reach out and grab the goodies.

25. Forget putting your old Frank Sinatra phonograph albums out on a wire to block squirrels. Records are much too small to stop squirrels. Squirrels seem to be attracted to records. Many homeowners who have tried this method of squirrel blocking have discovered that their squirrels can and will carry a tune. No one seems to know what they do with the records, but some squirrels must have quite a collection.

26. Send your squirrels to Rosie O'Donnell's home in Connecticut.

27. Two-part, spring-loaded poles, in which a spring-

loaded section slides down to keep squirrels from reaching feeders, will scare a squirrel—once! After the first ride, a squirrel learns to ride down the pole, waits until it bottoms out, then jumps to the feeder. This device often jams in cold and icy weather.

28. Install carpet nail strips on your squirrel's favorite place setting at the feeder.

29. Try prayer.

30. Keeping squirrels busy is one way to keep them out of your hair. Collect acorns and other nut crops in the fall and put them out in the winter for your squirrels. They will stay so busy burying nuts that they won't have time to eat your seed.

31. If you use a child's snow saucer as squirrel-baffling material, you must remove the edging. Squirrels will use the edge as a fingerhold and swing underneath to the feeder.

32. Researchers are trying to develop a synthetic form of tiger urine (because of the high sulphur content) as a potential squirrel deterrent. It will be so much cheaper than owning a tiger.

33. Spread dried blood, also known as bloodmeal, around the feeder. This Helter Skelter method might keep the neighbor kids out of your yard also.

34. Mothballs do not work, but some squirrels do not know that yet. You can try stringing up mothballs around the garden.

35. Buy a pack of cigarettes, trash it, and spread the contents on the ground around your bird feeder. Even if it doesn't work, you have done a public service.

36. Hot spicy tea, lemon oil, hot pepper seeds, dry mustard, and spiced vegetable oil are all concoctions that sup-

posedly will stop squirrels from chewing on siding and decking.

37. Put out a real owl that looks fake. Available also are fake owls that actually emit hawk recordings. That should really confuse your squirrels. The plastic predators are equipped with a photocell-activated recorder that stops screeching at night. These birds are so effective that not only do they scare all your squirrels away, you won't have any birds to feed either.

38. Fill the hummingbird feeder with prune juice.

39. If you have a problem with squirrels around the garden—compost them.

40. Plant land mines.

41. Drive hundreds of nails outward through the roof of the bird feeder, leaving no landing strip for squirrels to jump to.

42. Feed them a high-cholesterol diet.

43. Hire a dietary hypnosis specialist.

44. Place your bird feeder near the highway, or where your sixteen-year-old parks the family car.

45. Buy a bird feeder that suction-cups to the window and place it on the inside of the house.

46. Give up bird feeding if you can't take the pressure.

47. Design a rocket that looks like a tube feeder, capable of holding several squirrels at a time.

48. Put the plastic rings for the Yard Dart set around your bird-feeder poles.

49. Walk softly and carry a big stick.

50. Feed 'em and breed 'em.

Review and Relate

• When mama squirrels are lactating, they can be very persistent feed snatchers. That's right—the squirrel you like the least is a nursing mother.

• Squirrels spend twice as much time trying to get into bird feeders as people do trying to keep them out.

- Squirrels are ambidextrous. They can shove food in their faces equally well with either paw, which doubles their pleasure and doubles your feed bill.
- A litter of gray squirrels may contain both black- and gray-phase individuals.
- A squirrel will use mosses, grasses, and shredded bark to line the inner chamber of his nest. Squirrels looking for modern art deco decor will resort to the use of paper, bird feathers, loud-patterned cloth, plastic, and wood fiber.
- The squirrel is an opportunist when it comes to finding food. This gives him the option to live in a wide variety of habitats.
- One theory contends that if you leave your squirrels a water source in the garden, they will be less likely to eat your flower heads. This could be the new definition of a "squirrel chaser."
- In the wild without a large selection of suet, seed, and nectar to sponge off, it is normal for 50 percent of the squirrel population to die each year.
- Squirrels are the ultimate opportunists, and science is working feverishly to come up with a cure for squirrel visitation.
- When you see squirrels chewing on bones, even cattle skulls in the West, they are sharpening their teeth. They get a calcium boost when they find a set of horns. A steady diet of cattle skulls will make squirrels bullheaded and steer them in the wrong direction.
- Squirrels do not hibernate; they are insomniacs.
- The lack of enough "green corridor" forces squirrels to walk utility lines.
- Tree squirrels have larger ears than ground squirrels. Tree squirrels have eyes much bigger than their stomachs.
- A squirrel's tail gives him stability and many homeowners instability.
- Often, a squirrel will nip the germinating end of a nut before burying it. This way, if he remembers where he put it, it won't be a tree when he comes back.

- Squirrels can find nuts buried by scientists as often as nuts they buried themselves. This proves that squirrels can smell nutty scientists.
- There are albino colonies of eastern gray squirrels in Illinois, Missouri, New Jersey, Tennessee, and North Carolina.
- The nocturnal flying squirrel does not really fly. He hang glides using the wide membrane connecting the fore and hind legs. This membrane acts like a parachute as he leaps out and downward. He uses his tail as a rudder while airborne.
- Squirrels are live-bearers, not hatched from sunflower seed, as some scientists have theorized.
- For obvious tax purposes, squirrels often produce two litters in the same calendar year.
- Squirrels can move their jaws faster than a blender on the liquefy setting. They must stop chewing to listen for signs of danger.
- During the winter months, the fur of squirrels becomes dense, long, light, and soft. This makes for a very warm comforter.
- Fishing lure manufacturers buy tons of squirrel fur every year to decorate lures that bait their customers.
- An oak tree is an acorn that held its ground against a squirrel.

Tree Rat Trivia

THINGS YOU SHOULD KNOW ABOUT SQUIRRELS

1. What do you call squirrel thrift?
2. What gives a squirrel a wide field of vision?
3. Will squirrels eat birds?
4. Will a squirrel feed at night?
5. What is the most recognized mammal on earth?

THINGS YOU THOUGHT YOU KNEW ABOUT SQUIRRELS

1. Will squirrels share the same territory?
2. What do you call a squirrel's leafy nest?
3. How should you treat mangy squirrels?
4. Why do squirrels chew on high-voltage power lines?
5. What is the average weight of a squirrel?

THINGS YOU WISH YOU NEVER KNEW ABOUT SQUIRRELS

1. How many sunflower seeds can a squirrel stuff in his cheeks?
2. Why do so many people who feed birds dislike squirrels?
3. Will plastic-domed feeders foil furballs?
4. What does the U.S. Navy use squirrel baffles for?
5. What are the three most common causes of squirrel death?

Trivia Answers

Things you should know about squirrels: 1. Hoarding. 2. The eyes are located high on each side of the head. This allows a wide field of vision without moving. 3. If given the opportunity, squirrels will eat most anything. Before you get too upset, remember that birds also eat many squirrels. 4. Squirrels are most active during the day but have been observed feeding under the light of a full moon. 5. The squirrel with his signature tail. **Things you thought you knew about squirrels:** 1. Yes, that is why you have forty-two of them at your feeder right now. During the winter, they often share an apartment. 2. A drey. Some people who know squirrels well often confuse this with *dray*, a low, strong cart without fixed sides, for carrying heavy loads. 3. You can make them a toupee using brown shag carpeting or offer them flax-seed oil soaked in wheat bread and dusted with brewer's yeast. Spread some peanut butter on the bread to make it more appealing. Mange is often stress related, so you may want a slice yourself. This recipe will give your squirrels' immune systems a boost. 4. Some utility officials think squirrels get a charge out of it. Actually, squirrels feel a vibration in the wires, and they are intrigued by it. They chew through the sheathing to figure out the vibration. 5. The average weight before a squirrel visits a bird feeder is one pound. The average weight after a squirrel visits a bird feeder is one pound plus the weight of the seed in said feeder. **Things you wish you never knew about squirrels:** 1. Einstein theorized that by using the equation <compression x relative desire> the number could be limitless. 2. Because, unlike songbirds, squirrels eat larger portions and do not sing for their supper. 3. The problem with domed diners is that they do not take into account the lean, agile, athletic squirrels that can contort their bodies into extreme shapes while hanging precariously from the smallest piece of bark by one thin hair of the tail which has evolved over eons to hold the entire weight of a squirrel in a relaxed position for hours on end while eating. 4. Rat guards. They are used on mooring lines (ship-to-shore cables) to keep rats from climbing aboard ship. They don't work for the navy either. 5. The first is vehicular homicide, then predators, and—last but not least—overindulgence.

"Okay, move the feeder up another foot. I want to
try 19' 6" for the record."

CHAPTER FIVE

Homegrown Squirrel-Feeding Projects

Well, we've tried baffling them, we've tried scaring them, now it's time to learn how to live with and even feed them.

It is very difficult to keep pesky little songbirds off your squirrel feeders, but you have to try. Buying specially designed squirrel feeders will help you distribute seed to your squirrels and discourage the persistent feather dusters that think they own the backyard commissary. Mammals have to work together. Having a strategy that your squirrels comprehend and your songbirds do not is the first step to operating a successful squirrel-feeding program.

Squirrel feeders come in all shapes and sizes. What you should look for is the strength factor. The best are food-storage containers with hinged lids. The squirrels are able to lift the lids and take what food they like. A bird finds this lid a roadblock. Most birds do not have the muscle power to lift the lid.

Place nuts in a hinged box. It can be entertaining to watch a squirrel come up, sit on the hinged lid, and try to pry open the top and steal a nut. Finally, a little light comes on in his brain, and he realizes he has to get the lid off to be able to open it. Some squirrels will sit at the boxes and eat each nut they recover. Some, depending on how many nuts they have had to eat already, will take the nuts and bury them somewhere.

You can chase birds off your squirrel feeders, but they just fly in a holding pattern until you go back into the house. Then they are back doing touch-and-goes on the feeders again.

Anything you can anchor down, a squirrel can pry loose and a bird cannot.

There is a whole array of squirrel-feeding toys on the market. You can even make some of them yourself at home. One of the first was a "Whirl Your Squirrel" device. It was designed like an airplane prop with three arms that spun on an axle. At the end of each arm was a spike to mount a cob of corn. When the squirrel climbed to the top cob, the arm would drop to the bottom position and deposit the squirrel on the ground. This was an attempt to feed squirrels and still get the sadistic satisfaction of watching them get frustrated with their meal. It didn't take squirrels long to figure out the best way to mount this gravitational food tray was to climb to the bottom cob first.

There is also the slot-machine squirrel feeder. Every squirrel will gamble on this one. It is designed and built from PVC pipe. The squirrel can see the seed, but it does not come down to the seed outlet until the squirrel pulls on the handle that releases a few kernels of corn. At first this happens by accident, but soon the squirrel learns that putting weight on the arm means a reward of food.

Squirrel food can also come in block form, as a combination of nuts and corn and seed held together with a gum binder and placed in an ordinary suet basket. And let's not forget squirrel fishing. People have now started trolling for squirrels. You tie a peanut on the end of your fishing line and cast it out into the yard. When a squirrel is attracted to it, you wait for him to pounce on it, then reel him in. The squirrel usually does not release his grip until he absolutely has to. It's a great way to spend the whole afternoon, and you don't need a license or a boat.

You can try placing all these squirrel toys and feeders out in the yard away from your bird feeders in hopes of keeping the squirrels preoccupied and away from your songbird feeders. But don't put a lot of faith in fooling them for long. They still remember where the good stuff is.

Squirrels will use the birdbath as a water source. I have also seen them running through the sprinkler. All backyard wildlife will be attracted to your area by a good water source.

The first in a long line of squirrel feeders was a corncob table and chair, designed with a spike protruding from the table so that the cob could be anchored to the table. The most convenient way for the squirrel to get to the corn is to sit on the chair.

There is a shortage of corncobs available for the production of corncob pipes now that squirrels are gobbling up the grain by the trainload. Although most corn grown in North America is for grain and/or silage, at least one hybrid variety is grown for making corncob pipes. A cob should be at best one and a half inches in diameter and long enough to make at least two bowls (two inches each). The diameter of the cob should be relatively uniform. Pipe cobs should be woody and sufficiently hard to keep smoking tobacco from burning through the bowl.

Luckily, as squirrel-feeding popularity has grown, corncob pipe smoking has dropped. First corncob pipe smoking was banned in all government buildings, then in restaurants. Now secondhand smoke from corncob pipes is being blamed for myriad medical problems. In a round-about way, squirrels may be improving the health statistics in North America, even taking into account the stress factor squirrels cause.

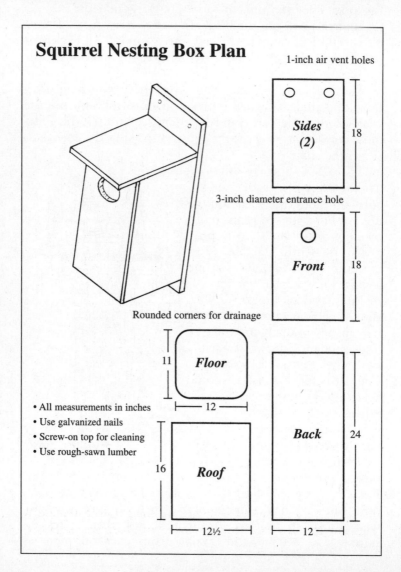

Squirrel Nesting Box Plan

1-inch air vent holes

Sides (2)   18

3-inch diameter entrance hole

Front   18

Rounded corners for drainage

11   *Floor* |— 12 —|

- All measurements in inches
- Use galvanized nails
- Screw-on top for cleaning
- Use rough-sawn lumber

16   *Roof* |— 12½ —|

Back   24 |— 12 —|

A well-designed squirrel nesting box is large enough for a family of five. Like building a nesting box for birds, using a high entrance hole protects the squirrels from the arms of predators. Make a screw-on top for easy cleaning and/or inspection.

Review and Relate

• You can also offer your squirrel nectar water. If not, you might find him showing up at the nectar feeder you put out for your birds. One part sugar plus six parts water mixed well should make your squirrel's sweet tooth happy.

"I'll have a Shirley Temple, and she wants a sugar and water."

• The male squirrel takes twice as long as the female to groom himself. Squirrels are the cleanest animal in the rodent family.

- When a squirrel senses danger, his first instinct is to freeze. Only his eyeballs move. When he sees you grab the broom, he heads for the trees. If he is already in a tree, he circles to the other side of the trunk, flattens his body to the bark, and peeks around to see if you are charging or bluffing.
- A squirrel will leave a scent on anything he buries. Some researchers say this helps him relocate his cache, even under a foot of snow or on another squirrel's breath.
- The average adult squirrel needs about a pound of food a week to maintain an active lifestyle. To lead an inactive lifestyle, he usually eats a pound of birdseed per hour.
- Squirrels chew on power lines to sharpen and clean their teeth. Talk about an electric toothbrush!
- Like humans, squirrels are either right- or left-handed.
- If you offer squirrels their own feeder with their favorite foods available, you can still expect to find them on your bird feeder, getting into trouble looking for and storing food where they shouldn't.
- No matter how reliable your food source is for squirrels, you will still find them hauling off a good share of the bounty to bury.
- Squirrel jaws have two actions. One, the lower jaw is pulled forward so that the upper and lower incisors meet for gnawing. Two, the lower jaw is withdrawn so that the cheek teeth can grind up food in a circular motion.
- In Britain a solution of copper naphthenate in linseed oil is used to keep squirrels off wood shingles.
- Offer squirrels a water source, even on the coldest winter days.
- As far back as records indicate, squirrels have been a sought-after game animal. During the Middle Ages, men bought their wives squirrel-fur coats.
- Insecticide residues are found in squirrel meat. You are what you eat.
- When chased by a dog, a squirrel runs low to the ground. This is called the mutt strut. A dog lowers his head during

the chase. A squirrel runs under a low object and drives the dog headlong into the object. So feed your squirrels, kiss your daffodils good-bye, and buy your dog a bike helmet.

- It is still not totally understood by researchers how a squirrel can hold all those dry, weightless leaves together when building a nest in a windy treetop. A squirrel stitches the nest together with twigs and hopes the building code inspector doesn't show up.

- Flying squirrels are the smallest tree squirrels. While most squirrels live alone, flying squirrels live in colonies known as squadrons.

- Use bluebird-sized nest boxes for flying squirrels and wood duck–sized houses for gray and fox squirrels.

- Spring breeding depends heavily on the quantity and quality of food available during the autumn and winter.

- Squirrels are not perfect. They often have ticks, fleas, chiggers, and warty growths. But remember, beauty is only skin deep.

- Man, through habitat destruction, has been the most serious threat to squirrels, rather than any disease, parasite, or natural predator.

- The word *squirrel-proof* in the dictionary is defined as "an illusion that one has been successful in preventing a fur-bearing seed eater from gaining grain from a baffled seed dispenser."

- When a squirrel digs a hole to bury his nuts, he will fill it with loose dirt and then pack it down with his front paws. Before he leaves the spot, he covers it with loose grass or leaves. He does such a great job, it is very seldom he ever finds it again.

- Squirrels are very vocal. Barking, chattering, screaming, mewing, and purring are just a few of the noises you will hear come out of your rodent.

- With the exception of Australia and New Zealand, squirrels are found on all parts of the globe. They are found in the coldest north and the hottest south.

Tree Rat Trivia

THINGS YOU SHOULD KNOW ABOUT SQUIRRELS

1. What is the average life span of a squirrel in the wild?
2. What causes balding in squirrels?
3. Will a tree squirrel live in a burrow?
4. Why do squirrels prefer to eat in trees?

THINGS YOU THOUGHT YOU KNEW ABOUT SQUIRRELS

1. What do squirrels look for in the middle of a paved road?
2. Are squirrels the only animals that hoard food?
3. How does a squirrel spend most of his day?
4. What does the Finnish word *raha* mean?

THINGS YOU WISH YOU NEVER KNEW ABOUT SQUIRRELS

1. Will plastic squirrels keep birds away from my feeders?
2. Do squirrels use sign language?
3. What is a camel-hair paintbrush made from?
4. How did Native Americans use squirrels in the sixteenth century?

Trivia Answers

Things you should know about squirrels: 1. The average life span for a squirrel in the wild is about eighteen months. 2. Mange, or scabies, is a skin condition that causes bald spots on squirrels. It normally occurs more in late winter and early spring and is not as severe in healthy animals with a good food supply. 3. Yes, a tree squirrel has been observed in extremely cold weather living in abandoned burrows. 4. They are less vulnerable to predators; it enhances predator detection and eases their escape. **Things you thought you knew about squirrels:** 1. Squirrels like road salt. They often end up licking their wounds after licking road salt. 2. No, many types of animals hoard or cache food, ranging from mammals to birds and insects. 3. A squirrel spends the biggest percentage of his day foraging and feeding. 4. *Raha* is the Finnish word for "money," but originally it meant the pelt of the red squirrel, which was once used to pay taxes in Finland. **Things you wish you never knew about squirrels:** 1. Yes. If you have a bunch of pesky birds eating your squirrel food, put out a plastic squirrel to scare them away. 2. Absolutely. Olfactory communication is used often by squirrels. For example, squirrels leave scent marks, using urine, throughout their home range for other squirrels to heed. 3. Squirrel fur. 4. To barter with the French and British for weapons, textiles, and firewater.

CHAPTER SIX

Rodent Rations

To feed or not to feed—that is the question. Feeding too much junk food to squirrels will often kill them—especially ground squirrels that semihibernate during the winter and rely on their stored body fat to get them from slumber to slumber. A park ranger in Glacier National Park once warned a family from Chicago, in a rented motor home, several times not to feed the chipmunks. The group didn't pay much attention. Whenever the ranger was out of sight, they could not resist the little beggars.

The chipmunks, having gorged on chocolate chip cookies all summer, must have known they weren't going to make it through a tough Montana winter. When the family packed up to leave, two of them climbed on board. They must have been sleeping off their heavy dose of dough for a couple days along the frame somewhere. They woke up on I-80, just outside of Chicago, and the two of them decided to play tag. They came screaming out of nowhere and running everywhere. The father couldn't get that rig pulled over fast enough. Everyone bailed out. They cautiously went back in and searched the whole rig but could find Chip and Dale nowhere in sight. Finally, they all climbed back in, two hours later returning the coach to the rental company without mentioning a word.

Opportunists. As we've seen, squirrels turn to a wide variety of food items when necessary. Normally they stick to a few basic menu items like tree seeds, fruit, and fungi. When their normal fare is fairly scarce, they quickly switch to foraging for whatever is edible. A shortage of desired food sources drives squirrels to rely on buds, new growth shoots from plant material, flowers, bark, and even lichens; that is when you notice young birds and eggs in nests missing. Squirrels do not make a habit of raiding birds' nests. If that were the case, there would be much more widespread damage to nestlings than actually occurs. As a possible source of roughage, squirrels will even eat dirt!

When food is abundant, squirrels will hide, hoard, and cache large amounts of food. If they do not, the food will disappear before the squirrels can make use of it. This practice allows the squirrels to extend the period of food availability. Taking advantage of your offerings to wild birds also extends the period of food availability. Work with the squirrels you have. Negotiate a settlement that will satisfy both parties. Go to the table with something to bargain with. You'll offer corn. They will counter with hulled sunflower chips. You counter their counter with a good mix. They will counter your countered counter with black oil sunflower.

Now it's time for a mediator! Ask your feed dealer if he can mix you a cracked corn and black oil mix with a few peanuts thrown in. Use this as your final offer and threaten a lockout if they don't take it. Trust me—they'll take it!

A hard nut to crack. Practice and good training are all part of being a successful squirrel. Studies in complex behavior patterns have come a long way in helping us to understand nature to some degree. In the case of the squirrel, these studies have shown us something about his nut-cracking techniques. This skill is both internally and externally developed in a squirrel. If you watch an older, experienced squirrel with a hard-shelled nut, the animal will take the nut in hand, examine it carefully, then begin to gnaw at the groove between the shell halves. After deepening the groove, the squirrel rotates the nut in his paws and bites down hard, cracking it wide open. This is a very efficient method of nut cracking, but it does not necessarily come natural to a squirrel. If you watch young squirrels, they look like they know what they are doing but often have not mastered the skill. They spend a lot of time gnawing the nuts, but not strategically. It is not until the young squirrels begin to listen to their parents, and take from them the examples set forth, that their eyes are finally opened to the realization that they still have a lot to learn and that parents aren't always as stupid as they look.

Parking your squirrel. Squirrels love to live in parks because people won't talk to them in the park like they do at home. People can cut through the park on their way home from church and feed the cute little buggers and talk gently to them. They even try to get the squirrels to eat out of their hands. As soon as these same people get home and see a squirrel on the bird feeder, they forget everything the preacher told them and blue profanity flows from their voice boxes as they attack with brooms. There is some ancient territorial trait at work here in the human spirit that is ignited by the presence of a nut-eating rodent.

Squirrels in a nutshelf. To a squirrel, the world is one big smorgasbord. Raw or roasted, peanuts are a gourmet treat to him, though some people contend that too many raw peanuts can be harmful. A straight diet of raw peanuts will not only bore a squirrel to death, it might even give him long-term health problems. Studies indicate that too many peanuts will actually cause malnutrition in squirrel populations by inhibiting the pancreas's production of an enzyme essential for the absorption of protein by the intestine. The best peanut for a squirrel is one roasted. Roasting for twenty to thirty minutes will usually destroy the inhibitor, making peanuts a suitable squirrel snack. Feeding your squirrel raw peanuts is not going to do him in, but if you take him to a ball game occasionally and buy him a bag of roasted peanuts, he will be much healthier and much more well rounded.

There are squirrel feeders and other devices designed to keep squirrels occupied. I've noticed that most of them give out peanuts or have an ear of dried corn available. Dried corn or peanuts are not "bad" per se. But if you are going to make a squirrel perform for you, it seems only fair that you give him something decent to eat in return! Try smearing chunky peanut butter onto a tree trunk and see what happens. He will also eat sunflower seeds (hulled or in the shell) and cracked corn, as well as dried corn on the cob. You can also give him slices of apple or pear.

Let your squirrel eat beans. Peanuts, which are not native to North America, are not natural squirrel food. Peanuts aren't even nuts—they're beans! They are lacking in certain nutrients, and their flimsy shells don't make them good for hoarding. You can buy commercial hazelnuts. Squirrels love them, and they make excellent hoarding inventory. They are closely related to the hazelnuts found in the wild. You can also collect other wild fare for your furballs in the

fall and put your squirrels on the dole. Filberts can be expensive if you have to pay retail for them. So why not spend a few weekends out in the beautiful fall forest, foraging for your own?

Try giving your squirrels raw pumpkin and the seeds. This can vary their diet from your usual ear corn, bird feed, and suet.

Squirrels love trail mix. The perfect combination for squirrel trail mix is whole corn, unsalted peanuts in the shells, slices of bananas, pears, apples, and dried fruit. Combine these suggestions on a string, smear it with peanut butter, and hang it near a bird feeder.

Squirrels love peanut butter and jelly sandwiches. Try feeding your squirrels pieces of bread smeared with PB&J. Fold each piece up and tear it into small bite-sized pieces. Use whole wheat bread. You can also add a bit of brown sugar with a few currants and raisins mashed into the bread. This recipe will make your squirrels happy campers.

Ever thought about giving your squirrel a fruitcake? You have to do *something* with fruitcakes. Most people use them for boat anchors, but squirrels love them. You can also offer your squirrel individual fruit choices like cherries, grapes, apples, cantaloupes, and honeydew, along with seeds from all melons.

Attract squirrels to your yard landscape with food plant varieties like cherries, huckleberries, dogwood, persimmon, and grapes. Squirrels even enjoy poison ivy. Most nurseries do not sell poison ivy, but many people who have it in their yards are more than happy to give you all you want. Many of them will even throw in a dozen or so squirrels.

Mangy squirrels. If you have squirrels with receding fur lines, it could be a dietary problem or mites. Mangy-looking squirrels can often be cured by offering them peanut butter sandwiches laced with brewer's yeast. If their problem turns out to be mites, your scratchy little friends will work through it in time. Balding squirrels go through a lot of psychological stress. You may notice some of them letting their fur grow long on one side and combing it over the bald areas. In strong winds it all blows back, and they look like half a hippie. Try not to stare or even make eye contact in a case like this. Just offer brewer's yeast and hope for the best.

Squirrels have very sensible eating habits in their natural setting. According to some studies, squirrels will eat acorns in such a way that the embryo is not destroyed and the damaged acorn will still germinate into an oak seedling. The squirrel accomplishes this by eating only the top half of the acorn, or the growing tip. The embryo located nearer the bottom is not harmed. So in the case of squirrels, you can have your oak tree and eat it too. This seems to be true with only red oaks. White oaks spread more slowly, from acorns the squirrels overlook or forget. Some squirrelly scholars say that is as high as 75 percent of the squirrel's cache.

I am not saying that all squirrels are little Einsteins. They are such persistent foragers that once in a while they will collect unsafe materials. Many fires are started from discarded cigarettes. What isn't common knowledge is that squirrels will often pick up a lit cigarette on the side of the road that wouldn't otherwise start a fire and take it back to the nest, where it ignites dry nesting material. At a time like this, a squirrel is seriously looking for a water source.

Providing water. The most important part of feeding is to provide a clean water source also. Squirrels do not expect their own baths. They will gladly not only use the birdbath but on occasion take it over and scare everyone else out of the pool.

Some gardeners contend that providing squirrels with a water source will make them less likely to raid the garden bounty. The theory is that squirrels are attracted to fruits and vegetables, in many cases, for the moisture content. If you provide them with a water source, they will not be interested in tapping into your plants.

Cleaning feeders. Bird feeders should be taken down and cleaned once a month, year-round. The same rule applies to squirrel feeders. Drain holes in the bottom of feeders will let water escape that would otherwise stand in the feeder and rot feed offerings quickly.

After cleaning the feeder of old foodstuffs and droppings, use a bleach solution of one capful per gallon of water to disinfect the feeder. Rinse well and let dry before refilling.

Recipes for Squirrels

Fat Farm Special

2 parts vegetable shortening or lard
1 part peanut butter
1 part cornmeal
1 part sunflower seed, peanut hearts, or chopped nuts

Mix well and place in suet feeder. Best if used in winter months. Refrigerate unused portion. If using during the summer months, place out only what they will eat in one day. May also place the suet on a platform feeder or wherever your squirrels like to come and get their treats.

Mixed Bag

1 part wild birdseed
2 parts black oil sunflower seed
1 part cracked corn kernels
1 part peanuts (in the shells)
1 part dry dog food (pellets)

Put this on your squirrel feeder along with a cob of corn and some chunks of raw suet. This will be a good enticement away from the bird feeders, which have lower densities of sunflower seed and probably no peanuts, which squirrels love. Don't expect miracles.

I found that by putting out grape jelly, I could attract orioles. I also found it attracted all my squirrels. So I started making them their own serving of fruit salad.

Fruit Salad

A small dish of grapes
Orange slices
Sliced bananas
Cherry tomatoes

Mix in 1/2 cup of peanut butter and grape jelly.

Corn Pudding on a Coconut Shell

In a bowl, mix together 2 cups of water and 2 cups of sugar. In a skillet slowly melt a cup of suet or lard. When it cools slightly, stir it into the sugar-water mixture and add 2 cups of yellow cornmeal. This will form a soft dough. Approximately 2 cups of all-purpose flour will stiffen the dough to a consistency you can work with.

Cut a coconut in half after you have drained the milk off. Fill the coconut half with the dough and hang it out for your squirrelly neighbors.

The Bagel Swing

String a bagel on a long cord and smear it heavily with peanut butter. Position it so that squirrels must jump a few feet to reach the bagel. This will be a favorite feeder as you watch swinging squirrels cling to the bagel and eat away at their foothold.

Any wild bird recipe you have been using will make a squirrel extremely filled and fulfilled.

This is an artist's rendering of Carlos "Fatsoratso" Gambini, a known swindler, con artist, and flimflam expert. He is wanted for questioning in a case involving a bait-and-switch tactic. Last seen in and around New Jersey. He belongs to one of the largest crime families in the United States. His family is believed to have their paws in organized crime in every backyard in North America. "Fatsoratso" has a harelip all the way around and a 48-inch waist.

Review and Relate

- Besides destroying bird feeders, squirrels will irritate by digging in the potted plants and eating all the succulents, breaking down tomato plants to get at the green tomatoes, and digging up bulbs.
- Burying nuts is an instinctive trait for gray squirrels. Those raised in captivity will bury their first nuts just as professionally as a veteran park squirrel who has done it for a zillion years.
- The squirrel's habit of burying each nut separately is called "scatter-hoarding." Research indicates that the squirrel uses this distribution method because of competition from other cache-crashing critters. The squirrel covers a lot of ground to find food. When he finds it, he covers a lot of ground over it for safekeeping.
- In the spring, squirrels eat tree buds, tree flowers, and early seeds. These give them energy and key nutrients, such as calcium and sodium. Their craving for nutrients might explain the ghoulish reports of squirrels gnawing on tombstones—a grave situation to some cemetery-maintenance crews.
- A gray squirrel uses his jaws like a crowbar by inserting his lower incisors into a hole he has gnawed in a hickory nut and snapping off chunks of shell, a bit at a time. A hickory nut has almost twice the calories of the average bird-feeder fare.
- It is believed that a squirrel uses smell and memory to locate cached nuts. For bird feeders, he keeps a datebook.
- A squirrel digs a hole approximately two inches deep, then places the nut in and hits it with his front teeth. This sounds very unhealthy for teeth, but a squirrel puts his whole body behind the movement. The squirrel then covers the nut with dirt, camouflages the area, checks for loose teeth, and walks away, trying to look inconspicuous.

- No matter how much a squirrel eats, it never shows in his face.
- The squirrel's success has a lot to do with his ability to vary his diet from location to location and season to season. One was once observed rolling goose eggs, almost as big as he was, away from an unguarded nest.
- Some squirrels can harvest as many as one hundred pine-cones from a tree in one hour. These squirrels are known as coneheads.
- Before burying a nut, a squirrel tries to remove any fragrance that could cause a future food fight.
- Feed your squirrels unsalted peanuts. Salted peanuts can be killing your squirrels with kindness. Too much salt in their diet makes them thirsty. When they are thirsty, they will spend their whole day bellied up to your humming-bird feeder drinking sugar water. Drinking sugar water will make their teeth fall out. Without teeth they cannot chew holes in your bird feeder, and they will starve to death.
- To a squirrel the peanut is not a vegetable, nut, or seed. It is an hors d'oeuvre.
- There is a great misconception sweeping the land. I think it is born of advertising in an attempt to convince the masses that squirrel feeders will cure all your ills caused by furballs eating your birdseed. Think about it. Does a squirrel really know which free food is his and which free food is for the birds? I'm not saying he is stupid; I'm saying you are!

    Squirrels are going to go for the best stuff in the yard. They are known gourmands. The only way they are going to stay at your squirrel feeder is if you tie them there with stainless steel, nonchewable cable.
- When squirrels leave scent marks on trees, they often place them under branches to protect them from rain.
- When not on the go, squirrels will squat on their hind legs and manipulate food with their forefeet.

Tree Rat Trivia

THINGS YOU SHOULD KNOW ABOUT SQUIRRELS

1. What decides the population of a squirrel's territory?
2. Do squirrels hear well?
3. Do squirrels have thumbs?
4. How many fur coats does a squirrel have?

THINGS YOU THOUGHT YOU KNEW ABOUT SQUIRRELS

1. What is a fake burial?
2. What is it called when a squirrel jumps from the third story to a feeder below?
3. How many squirrels did Moses have on the ark?
4. What is the fastest-growing pastime in North America?

THINGS YOU WISH YOU NEVER KNEW ABOUT SQUIRRELS

1. How do you measure a squirrel?
2. What do you call the habitat of a squirrel shared with other species?
3. How would you describe a well-prepared squirrel?
4. What is face-wiping?

Trivia Answers

Things you should know about squirrels: 1. Food, shelter, and mates. 2. There has been little study done in squirrel auditory perception. It is believed they have sensitive hearing. One can hear the door of the house squeak while sitting on a bird feeder 100 yards away. 3. Yes, on each forelimb they have a thumb and a small nail. 4. Squirrels change coats twice a year, spring and fall. The molt occurs in a sequence from head to tail. **Things you thought you knew about squirrels:** 1. When a squirrel pretends to bury a seed but instead sticks it in his mouth when he thinks no one is looking. 2. A leap of faith. 3. Moses wasn't into boats. Noah had an ark. 4. Squirrel brooding. **Things you wish you never knew about squirrels:** 1. Hold it against the kitchen door and make a mark. 2. A community. 3. Fried, broiled, or parboiled. 4. Squirrels will wipe their lips and cheeks against branches. It is believed that they are using their saliva to mark their territory.

CHAPTER SEVEN

Squirrel Droppings

This chapter is for the paragraph challenged. If you process information better in one or two sentences, this is where you want to look for information. Here you will find facts about squirrels that are so amazing, I hardly believe them myself!

- When matching wits with furballs, it matters not how you play the game; it's if you win or lose.
- A squirrel climbed onto the Metro-North Commuter Railroad power lines in New York one day and electrocuted himself. That set off an electrical surge, which weakened an overhead bracket, which dangled a wire near the tracks, which tangled in a train, which tore down all the lines.

  The result: 47,000 commuters were stuck in Manhattan for hours, waiting for trains that were not coming.
- Flying squirrels travel about three feet horizontally for every one foot they fall when gliding.
- Squirrel population estimates are made by assuming one and one-half leaf nests per squirrel.
- Fox squirrels commonly carry food to a favorite feeding perch, such as a stump or low branch. These areas are conspicuous because of the larger amount of food debris scattered about them.

FRESH ROAD SKILL

I was peeking through the bushes,
I was peeking through the grass.
I stepped out on the pavement,
And I swear he hit the gas.
I quickly made a U-turn,
And hugged the shoulder tight.
All I saw was Goodyear,
It was a frightful sight!

I look both ways when crossing,
Then I run to beat the band.
But before I make the yellow line,
Again I bite the sand.

I really do not like to cross,
But the feeder's over there.
So I make another go for it,
And this time I don't care.

I do not look or hesitate,
Just close my eyes and run.
I hear him swerve, I lose my nerve,
This crossing is not fun.

The pavement's hot, it hurts my feet,
But I should not complain.
My grandad in the prime of life
Was struck down by a train.

The road looks wide from way down here,
And the cars look mighty big.
But I will twist and I will turn,
And listen for big rigs.

And when the traffic gets so bad,
The crossing I can't make.
I'll stand on the shoulder looking sad,
Hoping for a brake.

—DICK E. BIRD

- When squirrels raid a cornfield, the farmer can tell which species is to blame by doing a little detective work. A fox squirrel will harvest a whole cob and haul it off for processing. A gray squirrel will nibble the kernels from the cob and eat only the germ, dropping the rest to the ground as waste.
- Squirrels are the Johnny Appleseeds of the mushroom world. Mushrooms contain huge numbers of spores, which squirrels disperse through defecation without even realizing it. This can take several days over a vast area.
- Douglas squirrels love fresh pinecones. They will store green cones in moist caches to keep them tender.
- A red squirrel will cache up to a bushel of food items in one cavity. He also loves maple syrup. A red squirrel will tap a tree and lap oozing sap.
- The northern flying squirrel is a graceful flier. When this little glider lands, he pulls up at the last minute to land gently.
- The northern flying squirrel will usually have just one litter per year, unlike the southern flying squirrel, which averages two. The owl is this squirrel's major predator.
- Flying squirrels make sounds similar to those of night-migrating warblers. Housecats take their toll on these cute little nocturnal feeders.
- If you think you have problems with your squirrels, consider the people who feed birds in southern Asia. They have giant squirrels that can weigh up to seven pounds!
- Up to 3 million red squirrels are killed annually in Canada for their fur. They are one of the few squirrel species that see color—in this case, red.
- A squirrel was blamed in New Jersey for chewing through a garage wall and causing an electrical fire that destroyed an entire home. While the firemen were trying to contain the blaze, the squirrel was making hundreds of trips into the burning garage, saving as many of his nuts as possible.
- It was very upsetting to the folks of a small rural Pennsylvania town when all the small flags near the grave-

stones, in the town's only cemetery, came up missing. At first, they thought the worst: flag burners. Rumors started that schoolboys had taken them as a lark. No one knew for sure, until one day the groundskeeper found them all balled up in a thick spruce tree on the cemetery grounds. Inside were four small, naked, very patriotic red squirrels.

- A squirrel needs his tail as a counterbalance when trying to reach a feeder from a clothesline. He grips the line with his hind feet, dropping his tail off one side of the line and his upper body off the other side. If he fills his cheeks too full, his weight shifts, and he falls headfirst on his tail.

- NASA is studying squirrels, trying to figure out how they can eat hanging upside down and never experience motion sickness. Researchers feel they can learn a lot from squirrels that might help astronauts live more comfortably in space and work for peanuts.

- A squirrel entered an off-limits building at Fort Bragg. (Most squirrels do not need any additional training, but this one could have.) There were several attempts to capture the squirrel, but after a few days he bit into a blasting cap and ended his military career tragically.

- Ground squirrels often take up residence directly under bird feeders. They find this a very convenient way to stock inventory for the winter. Don't be too upset. This seed is eventually distributed to the birds—ground squirrels make up a large percentage of a raptor's diet.

- The weasel is the ground-dwelling chipmunk's chief predator.

- Juvenile squirrels who have not learned to cross roads safely and adults in heat who are blinded by love are the most likely to become roadkill.

- Black squirrels have been on the Kent State University campus since 1961. KSU's unofficial mascot is the black squirrel.

- The chipmunk is active by day. His diet is nuts, seeds, berries, and occasionally nesting birds. A chipmunk will

even eat a snake if one doesn't eat him first. There are
several species of chipmunk widespread throughout the
eastern United States and Canada.

- The gliding membranes of flying squirrels are furry flaps
of skin and muscle. Rods of cartilage at the wrists serve
to spread the membranes. In "flying," the squirrels leap
spread-eagled and use their outstretched, gliding membranes for gliding and their bushy tails for guidance.
Glides of over 200 feet have been recorded.

- A male squirrel can smell a female who is ready to mate
up to a hundred yards away. The male gray squirrel can
leap more than twenty feet and do many other stupid
things when he's in love.

- Unlike the fox and gray squirrel, who eat primarily larger
nuts, the red squirrel utilizes the smaller seeds of pines,
maples, basswoods, and elms. Rather than being buried
singly, these seeds are cached in large quantities in tree
hollows, stumps, and logs. Like the fox and gray squirrels, red squirrels will eat any size bird feeder.

- All squirrels have strong hind legs and well-developed
hairy tails.

- All squirrels are diurnal except the flying squirrel.

- Squirrels are primarily vegetarian and are noted for their
fondness for seeds and nuts. Some species eat insects or
supplement their diets with animal protein.

- North American squirrels have stronger teeth than European squirrels. The reason for this is most likely that
North America has tougher nuts.

- You can tell a western gray squirrel from an eastern gray
squirrel by the drawl.

- During mating season, a squirrel can fall more than one
hundred feet without breaking his heart.

- A baby squirrel weighs approximately one ounce at birth
and is about one inch long.

- If you trap and relocate a mother squirrel during either of
her breeding seasons, you will surely kill her babies.

"We'll show him relocation. Let's go to Vegas!"

- Leaving pet food out and unattended will attract squirrels and other rodents.
- If you hit a squirrel with a walnut, chances are nine times out of ten he will not be able to pick you out of a police lineup.
- A squirrel using your house wiring for dental floss can cause fire and other expensive damage.
- Bird feeders often encourage an abnormal population of squirrels to locate to a small area. This causes a housing shortage, which they solve by moving in with you.
- Gray squirrels have what is called spatial memory; they can remember where a food source is and remove it with a spatula.
- The only way to completely stop a squirrel from chewing and feeding on landscaping plants is to replant a species the squirrel finds unattractive or replace the squirrel with a species that does not find the plant attractive.
- In the arsenal of squirrel repellents are taste repellents like hot pepper, sight repellents like plastic owls, smell repellents like mothballs, sound repellents like ultrasonic emit-

ters, and action repellents like you and your broom. Like all arsenals, no one weapon can win a war. You must use your entire arsenal on squirrels before you can surrender with pride.

- Squirrels have strong claws on their fingers and toes. These are excellent tools for digging holes to cache their hoards. Their claws give them all the traction they need to safely speed through tree branches, circle tree trunks, and ensure firm grips on your bird feeder.

- Because of well-designed eye location, a squirrel is able to see over, under, around, and maybe even through his head. This gives him the ability to survey the area for any signs of danger and to continue to fill his face as long as he can keep at least one good eye on you.

- For all the problems presented to the squirrel, this is one animal that not only can survive the human population explosion but also thrive on it in some yards.

- Squirrels and rodents in general have incisors that grow continuously, as the blood supply to the teeth continues into adulthood. In most animals, the blood supply to the teeth is cut off and they stop growing. As a rodent wears down his incisors, the tips are replaced by new growth at the base of the teeth. Very few squirrels wear dentures.

- It is impossible for a squirrel to disfigure his face by stuffing his cheek pouches so full of seeds that his beady eyes bulge. A squirrel's cheeks are made from the same natural materials that spandex is derived from.

- If you see a squirrel in the road, slow down. A squirrel finds no challenge in a slow car and will not try any usual daredevil antics.

- Squirrels live by a curfew. They always go home before dark.

- Peanuts intoxicate squirrels and make them act silly.

- Squirrels are among the world's best-known animals because of their widespread range and presence around human activity.

- Special cables with protective metal sheaths that cannot be gnawed through by squirrels are now used by many power companies, but they cost considerably more than standard cables.

- Squirrels will not always stick to a natural food diet. When given the opportunity, they will eat pizza, french fries, candy, and any other junk food they can get their paws on.
- Squirrels have the sonar skills of Flipper, the keen vision of Road Runner, and the brilliant olfaction of Lassie. They just have a problem remembering where they put their nuts once in a while.
- The squirrel spends his whole life within about ten acres, unless you become his travel agent.
- Safety to a squirrel is height. When danger presents itself, a squirrel always looks for an exit that points up—usually a tree.
- Ground squirrels that congregate in social groups are called coteries. Tree squirrels are solitary animals, but when they congregate in groups they are called Mafia.
- Squirrels have bad karma if they play in the roada.
- The names *eastern* and *western* chipmunk refer to their distribution throughout North America. The little seed thieves under your feeder could be one of these brands, depending on whether you are an easterner or a westerner. The eastern chipmunk inhabits most of the eastern United States and southeastern Canada. The western chipmunk, of which there are seventeen species, inhabits North America from the Yukon south to Sonora in Mexico. The western chipmunk prefers the wide open range.
- A chipmunk stores his food underground in a labyrinth of tunnels and burrows. (That is why the foundation of your house is sinking.) He will never store food that will rot. A chipmunk hauls food to his nest in his cheek pouches, loose folds of skin on each side of his mouth that can each hold up to fifty pounds of seed. Oftentimes, a chipmunk will climb into a bird feeder through a small opening and fill his face so full of seed that he can't get back out until he spits up some of the load.

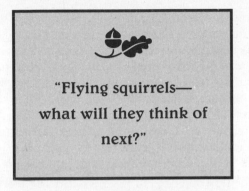

"Flying squirrels—
what will they think of
next?"

- Squirrels are the subject of many roadkill jokes, but in reality squirrels do not always turn out to be the victims. Hundreds of automobile accidents occur annually where the squirrel scampers off without a care and the car ends up wrapped around a tree.

- Oak, beech, and hickory trees are extremely important food sources for squirrels and offer a high carbohydrate diet for fat/energy production.
- Logging often removes mature timber that is important to squirrels as a food source and for the cavities the trees contain. Logging for firewood can be detrimental because dead trees containing cavities are often cut.

- Because flying squirrels are nocturnal and are not sought as a game animal, they have not been studied as extensively as other tree squirrels.
- Fox squirrels, who prefer open areas, extended their range into historically timbered land as the lumber barons began to clear-cut North America.
- President Coolidge had a pet raccoon, Rebecca, which he allegedly put on a leash and walked. This really made White House squirrels jealous.
- A baffle needs to be mounted high enough up a pole so that the squirrels cannot jump over it from the ground—at least three feet up.
- As wooded lots are cleared, squirrels are displaced from their natural habitat and forced to find new homes. Sometimes they will temporarily need to move in with you.
- In the fine print, many insurance companies add disclaimers about fires caused by squirrels. They will not pay on damage caused by squirrels, which includes fires caused by gnawed wires. Check your policy.
- Without natural predator controls, the squirrel population explodes. When development forces squirrels into metropolitan areas with few predators, excessive numbers of them survive on bird-feeder welfare, which only seems fair.
- If you want to hit a squirrel on a pogo stick with a water hose, you must point the hose six feet off the ground and fire when you hear "bong."
- Some squirrels learn to use their tails to hold open live traps while they eat the bait. When they have finished dining, they simply back out of the traps without being captured.
- Squirrels are creatures of habit, most of them bad habits.
- The red squirrel is more carnivorous than other squirrels.
- Most liquids, gels, granules, pastes, powders, and sprays that guarantee to keep squirrels away only keep you from squirreling your money away in your savings. Many of

them are harmful not only to the squirrel but also to other wildlife you are trying to attract.

- Baffles are sometimes more effective if not secured to the pole. A squirrel's weight can tilt the baffle and send him sledding off.
- When storing seed in bulk, use galvanized cans with combination locks.
- When putting up a bird feeder, use a very sturdy pole. There are bears in the woods too, you know!

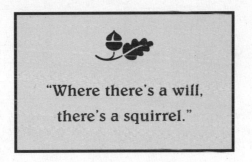

"Where there's a will, there's a squirrel."

- Besides chisel-like front teeth that can chew through just about anything, squirrels have well-developed jaw muscles.
- Feeders encased in wire will only slow a squirrel down. He will reach in with his feet and extract seed one kernel at a time if he has to, but he *will* eat your seed.
- Hanging bird feeders from thin steel wire will sometimes stop squirrels but will always kill birds that fly into the wire.
- Many bicycle riders report squirrels attacking them. Actually, the squirrels are just confused and many times get run over trying to decide an exit pattern.
- Of squirrel predators, owls, hawks, snakes, foxes, and bobcats are the most formidable, but they have never proven destructive to a squirrel population. These predators should be maintained to prevent overpopulations of squirrels and their diseases.

The not-so-meek shall inherit the earth.

Tree Rat Trivia

THINGS YOU SHOULD KNOW ABOUT SQUIRRELS

1. What is the squirrel's most common trait?
2. What is the hardest part about making a living as a squirrel?
3. What is a squirrel's most important birthday?
4. In 1776, where would you find most North American squirrels?

THINGS YOU THOUGHT YOU KNEW ABOUT SQUIRRELS

1. Why were squirrels so important to colonial Americans?
2. What are squirrel babies called?
3. If a squirrel is run over by an electric vehicle, does it die from electrocution?
4. What is a squirrel guard?

THINGS YOU WISH YOU NEVER KNEW ABOUT SQUIRRELS

1. How many squirrels does it take to break into a bird feeder?
2. Why do squirrels like peanuts so much?
3. Does the use of dog urine keep squirrels away from feeders?
4. How do you tell a fox squirrel from a gray squirrel?

The Hole in the Tree Gang

Trivia Answers

Things you should know about squirrels: 1. They're stingy. 2. Storing enough food for the winter. 3. A squirrel's first birthday is the most important. If a squirrel can survive his first year, the odds of a long healthy life (three to six years) are much better. 4. In stew pots or frying pans. **Things you thought you knew about squirrels:** 1. They could pay their taxes with them. 2. Squirrel babies. 3. No, from shock. 4. Squirrel guards are cone-shaped, flexible plastic devices installed on transformer bushings to prevent a squirrel from stepping on the metal connector and becoming part of the 12,000-volt electrical circuit. **Things you wish you never knew about squirrels:** 1. Three—one to hold the feeder and two to hold the woodpecker. 2. They are a source of protein and also contain niacin, thiamine, vitamins E and K, fiber, carbohydrates, many essential minerals, and a balanced share of calories. Plus, peanuts are cholesterol free! Though they do contain fat, the good news is, it's unsaturated fat—which is less likely to cause coronary disease than saturated fat. 3. It must. I never see squirrels around fire hydrants. 4. Some of the most distinguishing characteristics between a gray and fox squirrel are in the skeletal features. The gray squirrel has a smaller skeleton and tiny teeth located in front of the premolars of the upper jaw. After cooking, the bones of gray squirrels are white, while fox squirrel bones are pinkish-orange colored.

EPILOGUE

I hope you have enjoyed reading and learning more about the furball fraternity. You should realize by now that squirrels cannot live on bread alone. We need much more from you than that. We need love, understanding, respect, and kindness. But more importantly we need black oil sunflower seed, peanuts, corn, and grape jelly.

I do not enjoy being on a high-calorie, low-tolerance diet. I don't mind the high-calorie food, I just could do without the low tolerance to my persistence. All the bickering causes a lot of stress. Stress, as much as poor diet, is the number-one killer of squirrels and humans with heart conditions. Both the human and the squirrel heart would be so much healthier if it would just go pitter-patter with good thoughts every time we made eye contact.

When I was no bigger than an ear of corn, many people put out feed only during the winter. People would spring forward, but the seed supply would fall back. Today, that has all changed. Feeding backyard wildlife is now a year-round project that millions enjoy.

I happen to be a very important part of that backyard wildlife mix. It gives me a sense of pride knowing I have made an impact on so many lives.

I hope through love and understanding we can now

move forward into the twenty-first century in the spirit of reconciliation. With our hostilities behind us, the future will forge our relationship into a strong bond. Just don't let the birdseed run out!

One last point. I hate unsanitary bird feeders. I do not want to be known as Dirty Hairy. It's not good for me, and it's not good for your birds. I'll keep your feeders empty if you'll keep them clean.

—HAIRY HOUDINI

FRAUD-AMERICAN
LIFE AND CASUALTY COMPANY

SQUIRREL INSURANCE

This policy provides cash compensation in the event that the insured (herein ever after referred to as "the insured") should be subjected to harassment or rodent damage to said property as listed below the above:

1. All bird-feeding devices constructed of gnaw-proof material and not exposed to areas inhabited by rodents.
2. All suet products not left unattended for more than five minutes at any one interval.
3. All and any seed, feed, nectar, and nuts purchased for the sole purpose of feeding birds and pilfered by fur-bearing animals, if said foodstuffs are handled with proper security measures to eliminate any possibility of claim in response to any promises made or intent the insured might assume.

In the event of a claim, do not call the company. Wait for an agent to call you. Send your insurance payments directly to the company, since we save you money by not having any agents. Remember, with Fraud-American you can rest assured we have our best interest in mind.

GLOSSARY

M. A. Larkey's Squirrel Words

Arboreal—Living in or among trees.

Cannonball—A type of dive a squirrel uses to knock seed out of feeders he can't cling to.

Chickaree—A name, coined in colonial New England, imitating the red squirrel's staccato chatter.

Chicken—A game squirrels often play with automobiles.

Chubbyhole—A den big enough for a seed-fed fat squirrel.

Crepuscular—Most active at dawn and dusk.

Diastema—The David Letterman gap between squirrel incisors.

Diurnal—Active during the daylight hours.

Drey—A leaf-constructed squirrel nest.

Flying squirrel—Any member of two distinct groups of rodents that is able to make gliding leaps by means of parachute-like membranes connected on each side to his forelegs and hind legs.

Fuzzbuster—Any device that attempts to slow up a squirrel.

House—Funny-looking tree to squirrelly neighbors.

Hunch—The posture of a squirrel when he thinks he knows what might work to gain access to a bird feeders.

Hurdle-huddle—A squirrel meeting to figure out what has to be done to steal the seed in a baffled feeder.

Jaunty—The way in which a squirrel moves.

Jowls—The seed sacks on each side of a squirrel's face.

Klutz—A grounded squirrel that misses a branch while running through treetops.

Labyrinth—Chipmunk expressways tunneled under the bird feeder in the direction of your house.

Larderhoarding—Putting all your eggs and acorns in one basket and guarding that basket.

Liberals—Left-wing reformists who feel squirrels have as much right to the birdseed as songbirds.

Mangy—Scabby squirrels itching to get on a better diet.

Manipulation—Scheming to keep squirrels off feeders meant for birds.

Meek—Furry little rodents that shall inherit the earth.

Myth—The belief that manipulation works.

Nocturnal—Active by night.

Politically correct—Accepting squirrels for what they really are.

Posthaste—Hurriedly running up a bird-feeder pole before a squirrel knows it is greased.

Potpourri—The diet of a tree squirrel.

Profanity—Blasphemy used to keep squirrels off bird-feed stations.

Quarry—A squirrel during hunting season.

Quitter—Not found in a squirrel's vocabulary.

Racy—The obscene and indecent way a squirrel runs from a bird feeder with stolen seed.

Raving—The overexcited and irrational act of a squirrel's chasing a raven away from a food source.

ABOUT THE AUTHOR

Humorist and environmental advocate DICK MALLERY, aka DICK E. BIRD, publishes the *Dick E. Bird News*, a bi-monthly newspaper about bird- and squirrel-feeding, environmental issues, and nature—human and otherwise. Published in Acme, Michigan, the *Dick E. Bird News* is a tongue-in-beak account of the Best Darned BirdstorieS Ever Told. Mallery says it is the largest underfinanced, overextended "good news" paper in the world.

The tabloid newspaper covers a wide range of nature-related news from care and feeding of birds to dealing with squirrelly neighbors—everything you wanted to know about bird feeding but were afraid to ask. Subscribers to the *Dick E. Bird News* also become HUMMINGBIRDS— Humans Under Misguided Management Involved Nationally Googling Birds In Roost Dispensing Seeds.

For a sample copy, write: PO Box 377,
Acme, Michigan 49610,
or call 1-800-255-5128,
e-mail: wingit@dickebird.com.

I have been writing about the bird-feeding industry for fifteen years. No one ever tells me a bird story. Every bird-feeder story has a squirrelly character that plays a major role. Most people love to hate their squirrels, but over the past decade more and more backyard bird-feeder enthusiasts have learned to at least appreciate—if not love—their squirrels. Squirrel feeding has become an industry in itself.

You are not saving wildlife by offering food and water near your home. Your return on your investment is bringing animals in close where you can enjoy them. With that comes a responsibility to treat them fairly and humanely.

As we continue to multiply our numbers and divide our resources, we put increasing pressure on wildlife to find suitable habitat. Try to be more of a spectator and less of a referee when you deal with wild animals.

—Dick E. Bird